MEZE

FOR YIORGOS AND KYVELI——I HOPE THEIR LIVES ARE ALWAYS FILLED
WITH GOOD THINGS TO SAVOR AND GOOD PEOPLE TO SHARE THEM WITH

✳

MEZE

SMALL PLATES TO SAVOR AND SHARE FROM THE MEDITERRANEAN TABLE

DIANE KOCHILAS *

WM
WILLIAM MORROW
An Imprint of HarperCollinsPublishers

OTHER BOOKS BY THE AUTHOR

The Glorious Foods of Greece
The Greek Vegetarian
The Food and Wine of Greece

FIRST EDITION

Designed by Platinum Design, Inc. NYC

Photographs by Melanie Acevedo
Food styling by Corinne Trang
Prop styling by Kathleen Hackett

Printed on acid-free paper

Library of Congress Cataloging-in-Publication Data

Kochilas, Diane.
Meze: Small Plates to Savor and Share from the Mediterranean Table / Diane Kochilas.—1st ed.
p. cm.
ISBN 0-688-17511-2
1. Appetizers—Greece. 2. Cookery, Greek. I. Title.
TX740 K635 2003
641.8'12'09495—dc21
2002032881
03 04 05 06 07 ❖/IM 10 9 8 7 6 5 4 3 2 1

CONTENTS

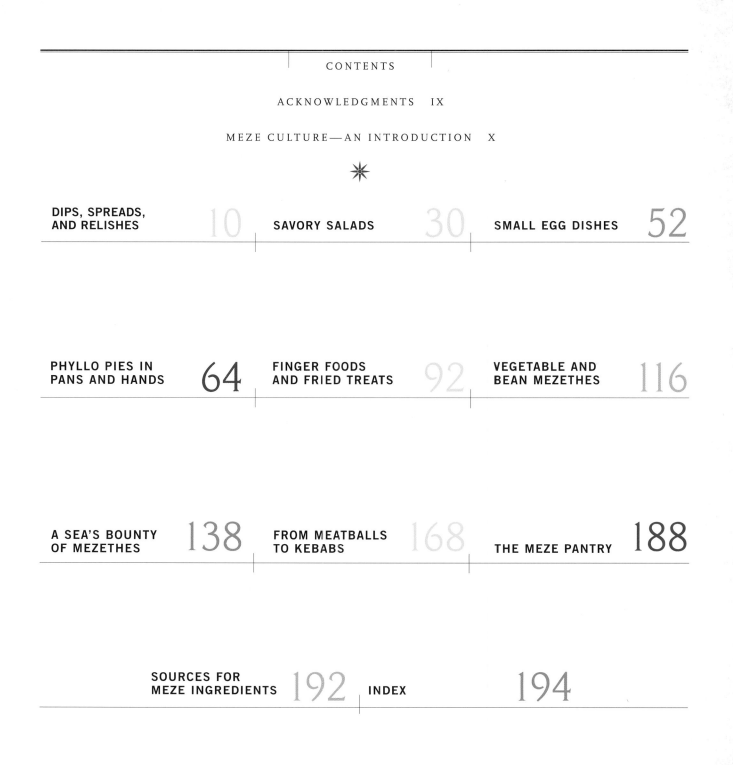

ACKNOWLEDGMENTS

I shared more than a few plates with friends, family, and colleagues while cooking meze feasts.

Harriet Bell, my editor, made *Meze* a feast to savor by spicing it up in all the right directions and paring it down wisely in others. Melanie Acevedo, photographer par excellence, made *Meze* a feast for the eyes. Doe Coover, my agent and friend, is always deserving of accolades for sharing advice and standing by during the highs and lows.

I owe special thanks to my friend and fellow cook, Brigitte Bernhardt Fatsio, who tested the recipes and offered up a few of her own for me to enjoy and pass along. I'd also like to thank Lefteris Lazarou, chef-owner of Greece's Michelin-starred seafood restaurant Varoulko, for opening his recipe files and sharing more than a few tricks of the trade. Special thanks to Sotiris Bafitis, a passionate Greek wine specialist, who helped me figure out what kinds of wine go best with mezethes.

The book's designer, Platinum Design, seasoned *Meze* with great visual taste, and Sonia Greenbaum proved that copyediting, like cooking, is a detail-lover's art. Thanks!

Finally, I always owe special thanks to my husband, Vassilis Stenos, a willing partner in conviviality and an able judge of what's good and what's not. I will always be grateful for having a loving family with whom it's always a joy to savor and share every last morsel.

MEZE CULTURE— AN INTRODUCTION

When I moved to Greece ten years ago, I had to switch gears from the frenzied pace of New York City to the more relaxed rhythms of the Mediterranean. I moved to Athens, a chaotic, bustling city whose charms take some time to uncover. One of the things I loved from the very start though was something I used to joke about, granted, with a little bit of New York sarcasm—that in the middle of every afternoon, throngs of people of working age, men and women alike from every walk of life, were crowded around small tables all over the city, clinking glasses, sharing plates, talking loudly in that lively, excessive way Greeks have when discussing . . . everything. They were doing what people in this part of the world have been doing for literally thousands of years—partaking in the trinity of food, drink, and dialogue (not always in that order), relaxing and socializing over a glass or two of wine or beer or ouzo and some savory tidbits of food. I was witnessing meze culture firsthand. It seemed much more civilized than "doing" lunch New York style.

In the eastern Mediterranean, there are special restaurants where you can go to savor mezethes. In Greece, they even have various names. There is the *mezethopoleion*, or general meze restaurant; the *ouzeri*, or ouzo restaurant; and the *tsipouradiko* or *rakadiko*—where people go for Greek eau-de-vie, called *tsipouro* or raki. A mezethopoleion might have slightly more substantial fare on the menu, and a bona fide wine list. Ouzo and Greek raki haunts tend to offer more piquant food, specifically designed to match strong liqueurs.

This way of eating—or rather socializing—was not entirely new to me when I moved to Greece. I grew up in a Greek family in New York, and on many afternoons or early evenings we had guests at our kitchen table, friends of the family who would come by unannounced and stay to chat for an hour, maybe for two or three. It went without saying that my parents, as hosts, even ad hoc ones, offered them a little something to drink—it might have been anything from coffee (an American habit they co-opted, but always with a food spin) to a scotch, to some Metaxa brandy, or ouzo, or wine—and with it something small to eat: bread or *paximathia* (rusks), olives, cheese, maybe a small bowl of taramosalata, if there happened to be some in the house, or maybe just a quartered tomato and sliced cucumber. These simple foods are the basics of the meze table.

The idea of food as a pretext for socializing is unique to the Mediterranean, and especially to the ancient eastern Mediterranean, in countries such as Greece, Turkey, Lebanon, and others. Although meze cuisine belongs to the general tradition of dining on a variety of dishes at once—on small plates, so to speak— meze culture is not akin to Spanish tapas or to French hors d'oeuvres or to Italian antipasti.

Mezethes (plural of meze) are not appetizers, and never immediately precede a main meal. Greeks have appetizers, too. They call them *orektika*. Mezethes are different.

The words *meze, mezze, maza, meza* mean middle, as in middle of the day or between lunch and dinner. Mezethes are almost always meant to play second fiddle to the drink at hand. In Middle Eastern countries, that would mostly be arak. In Greece, where there is a long history of viticulture, there are mezethes that are meant to accompany wines and others that match better with stronger drinks, such as ouzo and tsipouro or raki (arak). In general, mezethes meant for strong liqueurs tend to be robust and spicy; those that are meant to complement wine are generally a little milder. But there is no hard-and-fast rule. It isn't taboo to have both wine and ouzo or raki on the table.

The most important aspect of meze is that it is a cuisine meant not to sate but to tease. The whole point of snacking this way is to make the experience at table last as long as possible. The main reason for being around the meze table is to talk, to share thoughts with a few friends over a glass or two of wine or liqueur and something to eat.

Eating this way is a kind of game, and a civilized one at that, my good friend and culinary pundit (he's the Brillat-Savarin of Greece)

Christos Zouraris once told me. Savoring mezethes requires a certain discipline, precisely because you are not supposed to fill your belly as you would at a full-fledged lunch or dinner. "Invite three friends around a table. Place a well-appointed plate filled with four Kalamata olives, four hot pickled peppers, two salted sardines cut in half, and two slices of bread, also cut in two, and one bottle of the appropriate wine or good ouzo. If you can manage to keep your friends there for an hour, drinking, nibbling, and talking, then you have mastered the game." So he suggests in an essay he wrote on the subject about a decade ago.

*

There is an element of ritual in the meze tradition. In the small provincial port city of Volos, for example, within proximity of some of the best ouzo and tsipouro makers in the country, meze dining has evolved into a specific way to eat, so much so that in other parts of Greece restaurants open boasting Volos-style meze dining. The meze experience here follows a certain order, indelibly linked to imbibing, which is part of the whole experience no matter where one happens to be. In the most traditional of these busy restaurants, where there might be a hundred different dishes on any given day, you don't order. A specific meze, left to the chef's discretion, will arrive with your first round of tsipouro or ouzo. Another, different, perhaps more filling or more spicy, meze will arrive with the second round. As you linger, imbibe, and nibble, new and different mezethes are served, always one at a time, with each new round. If one meze is a small pie, the next one might be a pickled vegetable, followed by a dip or a bean dish or some fish. Variety, playfulness, and surprise are key.

The ritual of meze eating expresses itself in other ways, too, not so much according to the way restaurants have developed their menus, but according to the way people behave, their body language and mannerisms, while eating.

Once, for example, in a tiny fishing village on the island of Sifnos, I had descended with a group of friends to a place we were told had really fresh fish. The place was a picturesque hovel with two gas burners and tables whose legs were damp and rough because the sea washed right up onto them. In one corner, under a canopy of reeds and bramble put together to keep the piercing sun out, sat two of the owner's friends. They seemed permanently tanned, apparently from working under the Greek island sun for so many years. They were dressed in the well-worn kind of clothing that villagers never throw away, oblivious to the ephemera of fashions. They were also engrossed in a lengthy debate. One sat with his back to the wall with his right forearm resting on the table. This is the meze pose par excellence. Occasionally, he'd pick up his glass with his left hand, and use his fork to jab at a few slivers of fish that were fanned out on a plain white plate. His companion sat across from him, his back also against the wall, with his left arm on the table. Over the course of the two hours or so that we were there, they poured each other a few shots of ouzo from a small glass carafe, and they picked occasionally at the few things that the owner had brought for them to eat: four cucumber sticks; *tsiros*, air-dried small anchovies and an island specialty; and a small square of feta with three olives on the side. There was a little bread, too.

This is a scene I have witnessed so many times in so many small, forgotten places that I have come to realize that body language is as much a part of meze culture as the choice of simple dishes and strong, unctuous drinks. At a traditional meze meal, you don't sit facing the table, but rather facing the world and abutting the table with one side of your body. Why? According to my friend Zouraris, because it's not supposed to be a proper meal. The focus is on the social, on the conversation, on the exchange of opinions. Food is there just to facilitate that.

That is not to say, of course, that the food doesn't matter at all. Some of the best food in Greece, indeed in the whole eastern Aegean, is on the meze table.

Because they are meant to tease, the best mezethes have an element of wit and allure. Some of the most naturally attractive dishes in Greece are mezethes. They tend to be colorful without necessarily being artful so texture and variety are important. An array of mezethes should include soft spreads; crunchy, fried, or crisp baked foods; and both hot and cold dishes.

There is an element of fun in mezethes. This is lighthearted eating, a savory flirtation that can be indulgent just because it is not supposed to be very serious.

Mezethes have to have a certain snappy spirit. There are lots of wrapped, individual dishes; small hand-held pies; spicy, robust dips; crunchy fried foods; luscious baked dishes oozing with melted cheese; garlicky seafood and aromatic grilled meats. For an American cook, mezethes make perfect party food, excellent brunch fare, and natural offerings for buffet feasts.

The dishes in this book run the gamut of meze fare. Most come from the traditional Greek table, but some are culled from nearby traditions, such as Turkish and Lebanese cuisine. Some are modern versions of older dishes. All are accessible and can be prepared in American kitchens.

HOW TO PUT TOGETHER A MEZE SPREAD ✳

A meze spread is not meant to be a meal, but a nosh, a communal, convivial landscape of small and varied dishes perfect for grazing. Some offerings on the table might be store-bought, such as olives, cheeses, cured fish, or thin slices of spicy pastourma, the cured beef so well loved in the eastern Mediterranean. Pita bread or any of the Middle Eastern flat breads now available in the United States, as well as good-quality country-style bread, should also be on the table.

There is no hard-and-fast rule regarding what dishes work best together for a meze spread, but variety—in textures, flavors, colors, temperatures, and types of food—is crucial. There has to be a little of everything, from creamy dips to golden, crisp phyllo pastries, to refreshing salads to juicy meatballs or vegetable fritters, to one or two fish or seafood dishes, and richer dishes in small portions gushing with cheese and sauce. When composing menus based upon mezethes, a sense of variety and balance is the most important thing to keep in mind.

WHAT TO DRINK WITH MEZETHES ✳

Mezethes are meant to be served with alcohol, either wine or headier spirits such as ouzo, Greek tsipouro, and raki (grape distillates like eau-de-vie and grappa), and Turkish arak.

MATCHING MEZETHES TO GREEK WINES ✳

Greek wines have come a long way from bulk retsina. In the last decade they have gained wide recognition across Europe, especially in the prestigious British market, and they are finally making their way across the Atlantic. I wanted to provide general guidelines for pairing certain types of mezethes with Greek wines, and at the back of the book I offer a list of sites and contacts for finding fine Greek wines in the United States.

There are over three hundred indigenous grape varietals in Greece and two major trends in Greek wine making: Some wines are made exclusively with the noble, indigenous Greek varietals and others are blends of Greek grapes and well-known international grapes, such as Cabernet Sauvignon, Merlot, Syrah, and Chardonnay.

The majority of Greek wines, whether blends or not, are meant to be drunk with robust Greek cuisine, so they make natural partners for mezethes. You could, in fact, choose a wine first, and then go on to make a selection of mezethes to accompany it.

The two major red grape varietals in Greece are the xynomavro (xee-NO-ma-vro) from Naoussa in Macedonia and the agiorgitiko (A-ee-or-GHEE-tee-ko), or St. George, from Nemea in the Peloponnisos. The xynomavro is one of the most difficult grapes to master. It is believed to be the ancestor of the Nebiolo grape of the Piedmont, and it produces wines that are tannic when young and extremely complex when aged. A good xynomavro will have an intriguing nose, redolent of black olive, anise, leather, tobacco, oregano, rosemary, and thyme. A light xynomavro matches up very well to many of the egg dishes in this book, as well as with recipes that call for sun-dried or stewed tomatoes, especially when coupled with cheese, black olives, and foods that are redolent with Anatolian spices. Spicy meat dishes, recipes with pastourma, as well as cheese fritters, all go very well with xynomavro. I recommend xynomavro for almost all the kebab dishes as well as for the robust bean dishes.

The agiorgitiko wines, from Nemea in the Peloponnisos, are more giving and soft. You can often detect raspberry and other fruits in an agiorgitiko. These are good wines to match up with eggplant and with dishes rich in olive oil. They also go well with sweet and aromatic meat dishes, such as Spareribs Marinated in Wine, Honey, Star Anise, and Garlic (page 180) and Cinnamon-Scented Lamb Cubes with Tomatoes and Onions (page 181), and can hold their own against the strong aromas of pastourma, with its fenugreek-infused spice rub.

Greece produces many more white wines than reds, and here, too, single varietals and blends are equally savored. In general, most Greek whites tend to be acidic and citrusy and they go well with grilled fish and seafood.

Complex seafood dishes that are rich with olive oil, lemon juice, and garlic go very well with the wines from Mandineia in the central Peloponnisos, which are produced from the moschofilero (moss-ko-FEE-lai-ro) grape. The moschofilero is probably the most aromatic white wine grape, redolent of rose petals, with a beautiful, crisp finish. It goes very well with dishes that have mint and garlic, as well as with some of the seafood and cheese dishes such as saganaki.

Unctuous dips, such as taramosalata, and dishes whose main flavor component is sharp feta cheese go well with crisp, dry wines such as those made with the robolla (ro-BO-la) grape from Cephalonia or with the assyrtico (a-SEER-tee-ko) of Santorini. Both wines have a pleasant minerality. The robolla produces delicate, crisp wines with a lemon or citrus finish, whereas the assyrtico, truly one of the world's most unique grapes, grown on Santorini's volcanic soil, produces crisp, bone-dry wines with beautiful acidity. Most of the octopus dishes in this book are a perfect match for wines made from the assyrtico grape. Robolla or assyrtico wines also match up well with spinach and cheese combinations, such as the Spinach and Three-Cheese Triangles (page 72) and the Potatoes Stuffed with Spinach, Dill, and Cheese (page 130). The sardine dishes (pages 151, 154, 156, and 157) also pair up well to these two crisp island wines.

Another major Greek white grape varietal is the roditis (Ro-DEE-tees), which is produced in the northern and western parts of the Peloponnisos. The roditis produces wines that have a grassy, herbal quality and go great with almost all the salads here as well as with dishes that call for crisp green vegetables such as asparagus.

RETSINA

No mention of what to drink with mezethes would be complete without a tip of the hat to retsina, the distinct, resonated white or rose wine that is both embraced and shunned by wine lovers.

For decades, retsina was synonymous with Greek wines, especially with mass-produced bulk wines of inferior quality. Among an older generation of Greeks, retsina is still popular, but it has lost ground to the new, sophisticated, very well-made Greek wines that mark the industry today.

But even in the world of retsina, revolutions take foot, and there has been one quietly going on ever since a brash young wine maker named Yiannis Paraskevopoulos

developed an upscale, crisp retsina with barely a trace of pine resin and a crisp, clean character. Many wine makers are now experimenting with Greece's most traditional wine, and many new retsinas are starting to appear. These have nothing to do with the bulk wines of yore. An interesting light retsina is also produced by the well-known Greek wine maker Tsantalis.

The truth is that retsina is oftentimes the perfect match for robust mezethes, and one of the few wines that can stand up to many of the garlic-flavored dishes that Greeks like so much on the meze table.

SPIRITS

With the exception of the sweeter meat dishes and some of the more delicate fish and seafood dishes, all the recipes in this book can be matched with ouzo or with the grape distillates tsipouro and raki.

Mezethes and ouzo, the anise-flavored spirit that clouds up when you add ice or water, have always been perfect partners. Ditto for tsipouro and raki. Greeks have always made grape distillates similar to the Italian grappa, and in the last few years a few very talented distillers and wine makers have been producing fine quality distillates from single grape varietals. These, too, are increasingly available in the United States.

Vegetarian Platter

1 large hothouse cucumber

2 teaspoons red wine vinegar

1 medium, firm, ripe tomato

1 boiled potato, peeled and quartered

½ cup extra virgin olive oil

Salt and freshly ground black pepper to taste

1 teaspoon dried Greek oregano

Juice of ½ lemon

2 hard-boiled eggs, quartered

2 pita bread rounds, cut into wedges

½ cup Tangy Yogurt with Sautéed Carrots and Mint (page 14)

½ cup classic Greek feta cheese spread (page 24)

8 cracked green olives

4 to 6 pickled peperoncini peppers

I. Peel the cucumber and cut in half across its width. Cut each piece in half again, lengthwise, then cut into 3 strips, about as thick as a woman's index finger. Salt and toss with vinegar.

2. Cut the tomato into 8 wedges.

3. Cut the potato in half across the width, then in half again lengthwise. Toss with 2 tablespoons of the olive oil, the salt, pepper, ½ teaspoon of the oregano, and the lemon juice.

4. Place the cucumber, tomato, potato, and egg quarters decoratively around a medium serving platter or large plate, alternating between each. Spoon the tangy yogurt in the center to one side, place the olives next to it, and then spoon the cheese spread next to that. Place the pickled peppers around the platter.

5. Toast the pita bread wedges lightly, or brush them with 2 tablespoons olive oil and bake in a preheated 350°F oven for about 7 minutes, turning once, until warmed through and lightly browned. Tuck the pita wedges on the periphery of the platter, under the raw vegetables.

6. Drizzle the remaining olive oil over the vegetables. Season with additional salt, pepper, and the remaining oregano, and serve.

Seafood Meze Platter

Use the vegetarian meze platter as the foundation, but omit the tzatziki and the boiled potato. Embellish the vegetarian platter with:

MAKES 6 TO 8 SERVINGS

6 to 8 panfried jumbo shrimp (page 141)

6 to 8 Batter-Fried Mussels (page 110)

2 octopus tentacles, from the octopus with herbs (page 162),
cut into 1-inch chunks

4 to 6 pieces marinated anchovies (page 152)
or 4 to 6 pieces salted sardine fillets

10 to 12 Greek fries (page 98)(one potato, fried)

1/2 cup taramosalata (page 27), in lieu of tzatziki

Meat Meze Platter

Use the vegetarian platter as the foundation, but without the boiled potato. Embellish it with:

4 TO 6 GREEK MEATBALLS, PAGE 172

1 Greek or other spicy sausage, grilled and cut into chunks,
or 1 small dried sausage, cut into 1-inch rounds

2 slices smoked ham, trimmed, halved, and
rolled up into small cylinders

4 to 6 chunks Greek kasseri cheese

4 to 6 pieces sesame-covered feta saganaki (page 104)

4 to 6 slices fried preserved peppers
or breaded, fried hot peppers

DIPS, SPREADS, AND RELISHES

You have to understand the place bread holds in the heart and palate of a typical Greek to understand why the cuisine brims with so many different kinds of dips and spreads, in essence, relishes.

The practice of marrying bread with some sort of relish, and the practice of using bread as a utensil with which to gather up the relish, goes back to the farthest reaches of antiquity. It is a custom that remains embedded in the national psyche.

Relishes take the form of pungent dips and spreadable "salads," such as roasted eggplant salad—melitzanosalata—and fish-roe salad, taramosalata. Many of these colorful, robust dishes are among the best-known Greek food, fun to eat, and always present on restaurant menus in every dining category.

I decided not to include the absolute classics here, such as tzatziki, the well-known Greek dip made with yogurt, cucumbers, and garlic, and standard skordalia, made with potatoes or bread and garlic. You can find those recipes in every Greek cookbook, including my own previous ones. I opted to present dishes that don't stray that far from the classic fare but have a twist—for example, tzatziki made with sautéed carrots and mint, inspired by a Turkish meze; several versions of roasted eggplant salad, because eggplant is so versatile. Many of the recipes here are regional variations on the classics.

Almost every dip, spread, and relish on the meze table is turbocharged with flavor, from unsparing amounts of garlic to cayenne pepper to lemon. Their pungency is a welcome foil to the mild taste of bread, with which most are savored, and a counter to the strong liqueurs that these dips and spreads are usually meant to accompany. They make excellent party fare, and are easily matched with all sorts of other foods, such as bean dishes, roasted meats, grilled or panfried seafood, and more.

Spicy Tomato–Pepper Relish

The key to making this simple dish well is in the chopping. All ingredients should be cut into a fine dice, smaller than confetti but not so small that the pieces are indiscernible. This relish is a salad of sorts in that it contains a mixture of fresh, chopped vegetables, but it is eaten more like a salsa, scooped up with or spooned onto a piece of crisp pita bread. The dish is a classic in Greece's many kebab houses and goes well with grilled meats and chicken.

MAKES 6 TO 8 SERVINGS

2 large tomatoes, peeled, seeded, and finely diced

1 to 3 fresh chile peppers to taste, seeded and minced

2 medium red bell peppers, seeded and finely diced

2 medium green bell peppers, seeded and finely diced

1 medium red onion, finely chopped

2 large garlic cloves, minced

$\frac{1}{4}$ cup extra virgin Greek olive oil

3 tablespoons good-quality tomato paste

Juice of 1 large lemon

Salt to taste

Cayenne pepper to taste

Combine the first 6 ingredients. In a small bowl, vigorously mix together the olive oil, tomato paste, and lemon juice. Season with salt and cayenne. Mix the paste into the fresh ingredients. Transfer the mixture to a bowl, cover, and refrigerate for at least 2 hours and up to 6 hours before serving. Serve either cool or at room temperature.

Tangy Yogurt with Sautéed Carrots and Mint

This refreshing dipping sauce takes its cue from the Turkish yogurt dip *haintari*. In Greece it is often served in kebab houses and mezethopoleia run by Anatolian Greeks. The flavors are very robust. Serve the dip alone with toasted pita wedges, with ground meat dishes such as the ground lamb skewers (page 182), or with either of the two meatball recipes (pages 170 and 172).

MAKES 4 TO 6 SERVINGS

⅓ cup extra virgin Greek olive oil

2 medium carrots, shredded

3 garlic cloves, finely chopped

⅓ cup fresh mint leaves, cut into very thin strips (julienne)

2 cups thick Greek or Mediterranean-style yogurt or drained plain yogurt (see Note on page 51)

Salt to taste

2 to 3 tablespoons lemon juice to taste

Paprika

Fresh mint leaves for garnish

I. Heat 2 tablespoons of the olive oil in a nonstick skillet over medium heat and cook the carrots, stirring, until soft, about 10 minutes. Add the garlic and mint, and stir for a minute until the garlic softens and the mint wilts.

2. Place the yogurt in a mixing bowl. Add the cooked carrot mixture, salt, the remaining olive oil, and lemon juice. Place in the refrigerator, covered, for 1 hour and serve garnished with a sprinkling of paprika and the mint leaves.

Spicy Carrot Puree with Mint-Flavored Yogurt

FOR THE CARROTS

4 large carrots, chopped

$\frac{1}{2}$ teaspoon cumin seeds

1 teaspoon caraway seeds

2 to 3 tablespoons extra virgin olive oil

2 tablespoons fresh lemon juice

Salt and cayenne pepper or hot paprika to taste

FOR THE YOGURT

$\frac{1}{2}$ cup thick Greek or Mediterranean-style yogurt or drained plain yogurt (see Note on page 51)

1 tablespoon extra virgin olive oil to taste

1 tablespoon fresh lemon juice

3 garlic cloves, peeled

Salt to taste

2 tablespoons fresh mint leaves cut into very thin strips (julienne)

I. Place the carrots in a vegetable steamer in a medium pot with about 2 inches of water, cover, and steam over medium heat until soft, about 25 minutes.

2. Pound the cumin and caraway seeds together in a mortar and pestle.

3. When the carrots are soft, transfer to a food processor and pulse once or twice for a few seconds, to mash. Add 2 tablespoons olive oil, lemon juice, salt, and spices, and pulse a few more times to puree until smooth.

4. Place the carrot mixture on a serving dish and make a well in the center.

5. Mix together the yogurt, olive oil, and lemon juice. Crush the garlic cloves in the mortar with a little salt and add this to the yogurt. Season to taste with additional salt. Place in the center of the plate, sprinkle with the mint leaves, and serve.

VARIATION

Instead of the yogurt, try serving the carrot puree with a dollop of the whipped basil–lemon feta (page 22), or with a dollop of Spicy Whipped Feta (page 24).

Garlicky Yogurt Dip with Dried Apricots

This is one of my favorite combinations in the world. The origin of the dish is Turkish, but it is found in Greece, a rare treat almost always prepared by Anatolian Greek cooks. It is a wonderful accompaniment to kebabs and meatballs.

MAKES 6 TO 8 SERVINGS

2 cups thick Greek or Mediterranean-style yogurt or drained plain yogurt (see Note on page 51)

8 to 10 dried apricots to taste, finely chopped

3 garlic cloves, finely chopped

Salt to taste

Combine all the ingredients in a serving bowl and chill for 1 hour, covered. Serve immediately.

Roasted Eggplant Dip with Walnuts, Coriander Seeds, and Scallions

The Greek love affair with the eggplant knows no end. There are dozens of eggplant salads, dips, and spreads. Every taverna, every homey restaurant, every good cook has his or her own rendition and favorite. So many of them are good that I have opted to include a few here. The eggplant is perhaps the world's most versatile vegetable. Try serving this with some of the baked sardine dishes (pages 151 and 156), with the panfried shrimp (page 141), or with one of my personal favorites, the "breaded" sardines on page 157.

MAKES ABOUT 2 CUPS, OR ENOUGH FOR 6 SERVINGS

2 medium eggplants, about $\frac{1}{2}$ pound each

$\frac{2}{3}$ cup shelled walnuts

2 teaspoons coriander seeds

3 tablespoons fresh lemon juice

3 scallions, roots and tough upper greens removed, sliced into thin rings

$\frac{2}{3}$ cup extra virgin olive oil, preferably Greek

Salt to taste

$\frac{1}{2}$ to 1 teaspoon sugar to taste (optional)

I. Wash and pat dry the eggplants. Keep the stems intact. Roast the eggplants over a low open flame directly on top of the stove. Alternatively, you may roast them under the broiler, about 6 inches away from the heat source. Turn occasionally so that the eggplants roast evenly on all sides. They are done when their skins are charred all around and when they are tender to the touch, especially near the dense stem end. Remove from the flame and place on a cutting board.

2. While the eggplants are roasting, pulverize the walnuts and coriander seeds together in a food processor until they reach a coarse, mealy consistency.

3. To remove the eggplant pulp: Hold the eggplant from the stem end. Using a sharp paring krife, slit the first eggplant lengthwise down the middle. Use the body of the eggplant as your guide, and with the knife cut away the skin over both halves, as you would when removing the crust from a loaf of bread. The stem and eggplant pulp should be left, with the charred skin peeled away and fallen to the surface of the cutting board. Score the pulp lengthwise as well as crosswise to facilitate its removal. Using the knife or a spoon, remove as much of the seed mass as possible. Remove the pulp and place it in the bowl of the food processor. Pour the lemon juice over it.

4. Save 2 tablespoons of the scallions for garnish. Add the rest to the food processor bowl. Pulse on and off once or twice to combine. Add the oil in $\frac{1}{3}$-cup increments, and pulse to combine well. Taste the eggplant as you go. Season with salt. If the eggplant is bitter, add a little sugar. Remove to a serving dish. Garnish with the remaining scallions and serve.

NOTE

The eggplant dip may be made several hours ahead and kept, covered, in the refrigerator. Garnish just before serving.

Roasted Eggplant Salad with Feta, Onion, Peppers, and Garlic

I first tasted this lovely appetizer at one of my favorite Athenian haunts, the Naxos Cafeneion in Psyrri, a once industrial part of downtown Athens that has become chic and hip. The Cafeneion predates the neighborhood's gentrification and is still a place where Greek islanders come to socialize. On Sunday afternoons the scene is a madhouse. This simple eggplant salad is on every table, a much-liked classic for people to dip into while they wait, and wait, for the rest of the meal to arrive.

MAKES ABOUT 4 CUPS, OR ENOUGH FOR 8 TO 10 SERVINGS

3 large eggplants, about 10 ounces each

Juice of 1 large lemon

$\frac{1}{2}$ cup extra virgin Greek olive oil

1 large red onion, finely chopped

2 medium green bell peppers, finely chopped

3 garlic cloves, minced

$1\frac{1}{4}$ cups (about $7\frac{1}{2}$ ounces) Greek feta, crumbled

Salt and freshly ground black pepper to taste

$\frac{1}{2}$ teaspoon cayenne pepper

I. Wash and pat dry the eggplants. Keep the stems intact. Roast the eggplants over a low open flame directly on top of the stove. Alternatively, you may roast them under the broiler, about 6 inches away from the heat source. Turn occasionally so that the eggplants roast evenly on all sides. They are done when their skins are charred all around and when they are tender to the touch, especially near the dense stem end. Remove from the flame and place on a cutting board.

2. Using a sharp paring knife, slit the first eggplant lengthwise down the middle. Using the body of the eggplant as your guide, with the knife cut away the skin over both halves, the way you would when removing the crust from a loaf of bread. The stem and eggplant pulp should be left, with the charred skin peeled away and fallen to the surface of the cutting board. Score the pulp lengthwise as well as crosswise to facilitate its removal. Using the knife or a teaspoon, remove as much of the seed mass as possible. Remove the pulp and place it in a mixing bowl.

3. Squeeze the lemon juice over the pulp and toss quickly. Add the olive oil and stir the eggplant into the oil with a fork until all the oil is absorbed. Do not mash the eggplant with the fork.

4. Add the chopped vegetables and feta, and toss to combine well. Season with salt, pepper, and cayenne. Serve immediately.

Feta Whipped with Basil, Lemon, and Pepper

Feta is the Greek culinary answer to everything. Greek cooks savor their national cheese on its own, but more often than not use it as the base for myriad dips and spreads, or in fillings, stuffings, and gratins. This recipe is a not-so-classic rendition of the time-honored feta cheese spread called *htipiti*. It calls for basil, which Greeks do not use as readily as mint and oregano. You can use the dip as a filling for peppers, too. Try stuffing raw green or red peppers with the mix, refrigerating until the cheese firms up, and then cutting the peppers into rounds.

**MAKES ABOUT 3 CUPS,
OR ENOUGH FOR 8 TO 10 SERVINGS**

3 cups (about 12 ounces) crumbled feta, preferably Greek

3 scant tablespoons dried basil

1 heaping teaspoon cracked black peppercorns

2/3 cup extra virgin olive oil, preferably Greek

6 tablespoons fresh lemon juice

1 teaspoon lemon zest, cut into very thin strips (julienne)

I. Pulse together the feta, basil, and pepper in a food processor until combined.

2. Add the olive oil and lemon juice, alternating between each and pulsing after each addition, until the mixture is dense but spreads easily. Remove to a serving plate, garnish with lemon zest, and serve.

NOTE

The dip may be made 2 to 3 hours ahead of time and kept, covered, in the refrigerator.

Spicy Whipped Feta

This is one of the never-absent standard-bearers of the Greek meze table, a classic dish found from one corner of the country to the other, on almost every taverna and meze menu.

1 pound soft Greek feta

$\frac{1}{2}$ cup thick Greek or Mediterranean-style yogurt or drained plain yogurt (see Note on page 51)

$\frac{1}{2}$ to $\frac{2}{3}$ cup extra virgin Greek olive oil as needed

1 teaspoon finely ground black pepper, or more or less to taste

2 to 3 tablespoons fresh lemon juice to taste

I. Crumble the feta. Place it in the bowl of a food processor and pulse together with the yogurt until smooth.

2. Add the olive oil and pepper, and continue working the mixture until it becomes very soft and spreadable. Remove and refrigerate for at least 1 hour.

3. Just before serving, spike the flavor to taste with lemon juice.

Smoked Trout Whipped with Potatoes and Olive Oil

Cured fish of all sorts make their way onto the meze platters of Greece as perfect, pungent accompaniments to ouzo, tsipouro, and raki (Greek eau-de-vie). This dip can stand on its own with a few olives and some toasted bread or pita.

MAKES ABOUT 3 CUPS, OR 8 TO 10 SERVINGS

2 large boiling potatoes

3 large garlic cloves, chopped

3 smoked trout or salmon trout fillets, shredded (about 3 ounces each)

Salt to taste

$\frac{1}{3}$ to $\frac{1}{2}$ cup extra virgin Greek olive oil as needed

Juice of 1 lemon, or more if necessary, plus 1 lemon, sliced

$\frac{1}{3}$ cup finely chopped fresh dill

Freshly ground black pepper to taste

I. Wash and scrub the potatoes. Bring to a boil over high heat in a large pot of salted water. Reduce the heat to medium and simmer the potatoes until the skins have split open and the potatoes are tender. Remove, drain, and reserve 1 cup of the hot potato water. Let the potatoes cool until they can be handled easily. They should be warm.

2. Peel the potatoes and place them in a large mortar. Pound with the pestle. As they disintegrate, add the garlic, trout, and a little salt, and pound to combine. Continue pounding, and add enough of the olive oil and lemon juice in alternating doses until the mixture is smooth but dense. If the mixture is too dense, you can loosen it by adding a little of the potato water. Remove from the mortar, and adjust the seasoning with salt and pepper. To serve, place in a bowl, sprinkle the dill decoratively around the perimeter of the dip, and garnish with lemon slices.

Walnut-Garlic Dip with Yogurt

This is my all-time favorite rendition of the classic Greek garlic-and-potato or garlic-and-bread dipping sauce. The addition of yogurt brings it closer to the northern Greek and Turkish tarator. It has a rich, satisfying texture, an earthy flavor, thanks to the walnuts, and a light, soothing color. Serve it with Batter-Fried Mussels (page 110) or any of the squid, cuttlefish, or octopus recipes.

MAKES ABOUT 3 CUPS, OR 8 SERVINGS

Two 1-inch slices stale country-style bread, crusts removed

$1\frac{1}{2}$ cups shelled walnuts

2 large garlic cloves, peeled

Salt

$\frac{1}{2}$ to $\frac{2}{3}$ cup extra virgin olive oil as needed

3 to 4 tablespoons red wine vinegar to taste

1 cup thick Greek or Mediterranean-style yogurt or drained plain yogurt (see Note on page 51)

2 medium cucumbers, peeled and sliced into $\frac{1}{4}$-inch rounds

I. Run the bread under the tap and squeeze dry very well between the palms of your hands.

2. Place the bread, walnuts, and garlic in a large mortar and start pounding. Add a little salt and a few tablespoons of the olive oil. Continue pounding, and add the remaining olive oil and the vinegar in alternating doses until the mixture is dense and creamy. Transfer to a bowl and mix in the yogurt. Adjust the seasoning with salt.

3. Salt the cucumbers lightly. Place the dip on a platter, arrange the cucumbers around it decoratively, and serve.

NOTE

The dip may also be prepared in a food processor by pulsing the first 6 ingredients on and off until creamy. You must be careful not to overprocess lest the starch in the bread break down too much, resulting in a pasty, gummy skordalia. Add the yogurt separately in a mixing bowl.

Fluffy Fish–Roe Dip with Ground Almonds

There are as many versions of taramosalata in Greece as there are cooks who prepare it. Most are variations of the basic potato- or bread-and-fish-roe spread, a classic of the traditional Lenten table that has made its way onto taverna menus and become a Greek standard from Athens to Adelaide. The almonds in this recipe are a regional variation from the north of Greece. The "trick" of adding a little soda water to the mixture makes the otherwise dense and sometimes stodgy taramosalata light, airy, and fluffy. Serve this with raw sliced vegetables, such as celery stalks and endive, with pita bread, or with any other kind of bread.

MAKES ABOUT 2 CUPS

2 cups whole blanched almonds

1 small garlic clove, finely chopped

4 tablespoons tarama (carp roe), preferably uncolored

6 tablespoons extra virgin Greek olive oil, or more as needed

Juice of 1 large lemon, or more to taste

$\frac{1}{4}$ to $\frac{1}{2}$ cup seltzer water as needed

Pinch of cracked black peppercorns

1. Pulverize the almonds to a very fine grind in the food processor. Add the garlic. Pulse on and off about 5 times to combine.

2. Add the tarama and pulse on and off to blend. Pour in the olive oil and lemon juice, alternating between each and pulsing after each addition. Slowly adjust the consistency of the taramosalata by adding the seltzer, in 2-tablespoon increments. Add more olive oil or lemon juice to taste. The oil will help make the taramosalata creamier. The taramosalata should be as loose as a nongrainy mustard, although it will not be smooth because of the almond base. Sprinkle with cracked black pepper and serve immediately, or refrigerate, covered, for up to 3 hours before serving.

Navy Bean and Roasted Garlic Puree

The following recipe is my hybrid. Mashed bean dips, a popular meze in the Greek islands, are usually made with broad beans. Yellow split peas, pureed or mashed, are also a classic on Greek meze menus. I wanted a subtle, creamy white bean dip, with an earthy garlic undertone but with none of the harshness of flavor imparted by raw garlic, even though Greeks love that strong flavor so much. The result is this mild, filling version of skordalia.

It is delicious served with roasted or boiled beets dressed with a little olive oil and vinegar, or with broiled or grilled octopus (page 159) or fried squid (page 166).

MAKES ABOUT 2 CUPS

1/2 cup dried small white beans (navy beans), soaked overnight or according to package directions

1 large boiling potato, peeled and diced

Salt

4 large whole heads of garlic

1/2 to 2/3 cup extra virgin olive oil as needed

Juice of 1 large lemon

4 to 6 tablespoons white wine vinegar to taste

I. Preheat the oven to 350°F. Drain the soaked beans. Place in a medium pot together with the diced potato. Pour in enough water to cover by 2 inches. Bring the beans to a boil over high heat. Reduce the heat to low, partially cover the pot, and simmer the beans and potato for 1 to 1½ hours, or until the beans are extremely tender and practically disintegrating. Add more water to the pot while cooking if necessary to keep the contents from drying out. The beans should absorb most of the water by the time they are done. About 10 minutes before removing the beans from the heat, season to taste with ample salt.

2. While the beans are cooking, wrap each of the garlic heads in aluminum foil and roast in the oven for about 1 hour. Remove but keep wrapped until ready to use.

3. Remove the pot from the heat. There should be very little liquid left. Drain.

4. Place the bean and potato mixture in the bowl of a food processor, and pulse on and off to mash. Unwrap the garlic and squeeze the pulp from every clove into the bean-potato mixture. Pulse on and off, drizzling in alternating doses with olive oil and lemon juice. Adjust seasoning by adding the vinegar and more salt to taste. Serve either warm or at room temperature.

VARIATION

In Greece traditional home cooks have a different technique for drawing the pungency out of garlic. Instead of roasting whole heads, they poach them in lightly salted water for about 2 minutes. You may use poached, instead of roasted, garlic in this dish. Once poached, you can preserve the garlic in olive oil.

SAVORY SALADS

Greek salad is arguably the country's most famous dish, and is found on Greek restaurant menus all over the world. It's no wonder. The combination of tomatoes, onions, peppers, cucumbers, olives, and feta is addictive, and all the more so when the tomatoes are vine-ripened under the nourishing Greek sun, when the onions are the pungent red variety that Greeks use most, when the cucumbers are crunchy and the feta creamy and tart. All that coupled with excellent Greek olive oil and sea salt, savored with country bread, and it's easy to see why this simple salad is such a classic.

It is certainly not the only salad on the meze table. Greeks eat all sorts of vegetables, pulses, grains, even fish and meat as salads. Salads meant for the meze table, though, are usually more playful and dynamic. A meze salad should be able to hold its own next to the robust fare around it, to the dips and spreads, to the crisp individual phyllo pies, to the spicy meatballs, and more. On the meze table, a salad is something you nibble on and come back to.

Among my favorite salad ingredients is arugula, *roka* in Greek. It grows wild, but also is cultivated year round. In the dry Mediterranean climate, arugula becomes especially peppery and delicious. I like to match arugula with another traditional ingredient, one that belongs to the larder of the whole eastern Aegean: pastourma, cured beef seasoned with a spicy fenugreek-based rub.

A salad is only as good as its seasoning, and so much flavor in the Greek salad bowl comes from the excellent quality of the country's wild herbs. The two most popular Greek herbs are without doubt oregano and mint. Greek oregano is highly aromatic, and is usually savored dried, whereas mint is used fresh in the Greek kitchen. I call for herbs in many recipes throughout the book, and I strongly recommend seeking out Greek wild herbs (see Sources, page 192) to use in the recipes that follow. They have an intensity of flavor that derives from the bright, arid climate, and they make all sorts of dishes sparkle.

Greek Salad with Barley Rusks and Crumbled Cheeses

2 thick Cretan barley rusks or slices of very stale and hard country-style bread (see Note on page 34)

2 tablespoons extra virgin olive oil, plus ½ cup

Salt

2 medium tomatoes, cored and cut into ½-inch cubes

1 large red onion, chopped

1 large green bell pepper, seeded and diced

1 medium cucumber, peeled and cut into ½-inch cubes

1 chile pepper, seeded and finely chopped

3 small pickled green peppers, sliced into thin rounds

2 tablespoons small capers, rinsed and drained

⅔ cup (about 2½ ounces) crumbled Greek feta cheese

½ cup (about ¼ pound) Greek anthotyro, fresh myzithra cheese, or farmer's cheese

½ teaspoon freshly ground black pepper

1 scant teaspoon dried basil

1 scant teaspoon dried Greek oregano

12 to 15 cracked green olives to taste

I. Dampen the rusks under the tap, drain off the water and break into large pieces. Place on the bottom of a large salad bowl and drizzle with 2 tablespoons olive oil. If using the bread, heat the oil in a nonstick skillet over low heat and toast 1 slice at a time in the oiled pan, turning until golden on both sides. Remove and set aside to cool for a few minutes. Cut into pieces and place on the bottom of the salad bowl. Season with a little salt.

2. Add the tomatoes, then the onion, peppers, and capers to the bowl. Season with salt.

3. Using a fork, mix the feta and other cheese together with the pepper and a pinch of the dried herbs. Crumble the mixture over the salad. Toss the olives into the salad, drizzle with ½ cup olive oil and sprinkle with the remaining herbs and additional salt. Toss just before serving.

Bread Salad with Barley Rusks, Tomato, Mint, and Green Apple

Most bread salads simply call for tomatoes, herbs, and a little cheese. This version is not traditionally Greek, but one that we developed for our restaurant, Villa Thanassi, on the island of Ikaria. Refreshing and filling, it became our standard Greek salad.

MAKES 6 SERVINGS

2 thick Cretan barley rusks or two slices very stale, hard country-style bread

1 large tomato, cut into $1/2$-inch cubes

Salt

1 Granny Smith apple

Juice of $1/2$ lemon

1 medium red onion, cut into thin rings

2 tablespoons small capers, rinsed and drained

$1/2$ cup fresh mint leaves, finely chopped

2 tablespoons fresh oregano leaves

$1/3$ to $1/2$ cup extra virgin Greek olive oil to taste

1. Run each of the rusks under the tap or dip them for a few seconds in a bowl of cold water. Hold them up and let the water drip off completely. Break the rusks into large pieces and place in a serving bowl.

2. Add the tomato to the bread, tossing with a little salt. Peel and grate the apple along the wide-toothed side of a handheld cheese grater, working carefully down to the core. Sprinkle the lemon juice over the apple. Top with the onion, capers, and herbs. Pour the olive oil over the salad, season with additional salt, toss well, and serve.

NOTE

Cretan barley rusks may be found in Greek grocery stores across the United States and in some food specialty shops. You can make your own rusks by slicing country-style bread into 2-inch-thick wedges and baking on an ungreased sheet pan in a low oven for several hours until dry and hard.

Arugula Salad with Pastourma and Wrinkled Black Olives

Pastourma is usually served on its own as a meze accompanied by bread, cheese, and tomatoes, or used as an ingredient in cheese-filled savory pies and omelets. Here, the spicy eastern Mediterranean cured beef with the fenugreek rub adds an unusual and aromatic dimension to this salad.

MAKES 6 TO 8 SERVINGS

1 bunch arugula, stems cut off and discarded, leaves coarsely chopped

1 medium red onion, halved and sliced

10 cherry tomatoes, halved

3 slices pastourma, sticky spice rub removed from the rim

10 wrinkled black Greek throumbes or Moroccan wrinkled black olives

FOR THE DRESSING

$1/3$ cup extra virgin Greek olive oil

3 tablespoons red wine or sherry vinegar

1 tablespoon Greek thyme or mountain honey

1 tablespoon grainy Dijon mustard

Salt and freshly ground black pepper to taste

I. Wash and spin the arugula dry in a salad spinner. Place in a medium serving bowl. Place the onion on top, then the cherry tomatoes.

2. Julienne the pastourma, diagonally across the width of each slice, into short $1/4$-inch strips. Add to the salad. Top with the wrinkled black olives.

3. Whisk together the olive oil, vinegar, honey, mustard, salt, and pepper. Dress and mix the salad and serve immediately.

VARIATION

Add $1/4$ cup fresh orange juice to the dressing and reduce the vinegar to 2 tablespoons. You may also add a handful of the sweet-salty walnuts that appear on page 94.

Bread Salad with Watermelon, Feta, and Red Onion

The combination of feta and watermelon is one that Greek connoisseurs savor with special gusto. There is no recipe for enjoying the two together. Cut-up watermelon is served on one plate with a little feta cheese, or served separately and left to each diner to join the two together in a forkful. Here, I take this elemental duet and make something a little more special. Seek out the sweetest watermelon and Dodoni feta. You can find the latter in most Greek and Middle Eastern food shops, as well as in specialty cheese emporiums. The feta from Dodoni in Epirus has a firm, creamy texture and can be cut into cubes without crumbling.

MAKES 4 SERVINGS

1 Cretan barley rusk or 1 thick slice of
  stale country-style bread (see Note on page 34)

1 medium red onion, sliced into thin rings

3 cups cold watermelon, cut into 1-inch cubes

1 cup (about 4 ounces) Greek feta, cut into $\frac{1}{2}$-inch cubes

1 teaspoon sherry or raspberry vinegar

Freshly ground black pepper to taste

A few mint sprigs

I. Dampen the bread under running water and then hold it over the sink for the water to drip off. Break it into chunks, about 1 inch each.

2. Place the chunks on the bottom of a serving bowl and sprinkle half the onion slices over them. Place the watermelon and any of its juices together with the feta cubes on top. Drizzle in the vinegar and toss gently, careful not to mash the watermelon. Season with pepper and garnish with the remaining onion slices and mint. Serve.

Winter Greens with Caper–Sun-Dried Tomato Vinaigrette

This simple salad is robust and tangy.

3 cups finely shredded white cabbage

3 cups finely shredded arugula

1 large carrot, shredded

$\frac{1}{2}$ cup wrinkled black olives

FOR THE DRESSING

1 large garlic clove, chopped

3 tablespoons small capers, rinsed and drained

$\frac{1}{4}$ cup finely chopped sun-dried tomatoes

$\frac{2}{3}$ cup extra virgin Greek olive oil

Juice of 1 lemon

2 teaspoons grainy Dijon mustard

Salt

1. Combine the greens, carrot, and olives in a bowl.

2. Pulverize the garlic, capers, and sun-dried tomatoes in a food processor or blender. Add the olive oil, lemon juice, mustard, and salt, and pulse on and off until emulsified. Pour the dressing over the salad just before serving.

Arugula and Shaved Fennel Salad with Nigella and Manouri Cheese

Greek arugula is extremely peppery and delicious. The fennel is cooling, the mild manouri cheese soothing, and the nigella—"black sesame," as the Greeks euphemistically refer to it—adds a delicious, smoky crunch. Together, they work really well.

MAKES 6 TO 8 SERVINGS

½ large fennel bulb, cut into paper-thin slices (about 3 cups)

½ cup extra virgin Greek olive oil

2 to 3 tablespoons red wine vinegar to taste

2 tablespoons fresh orange juice

Salt and freshly ground black pepper to taste

4 cups trimmed, torn arugula leaves

3½-inch round slices of Greek manouri cheese or ricotta salata (about 6 ounces)

1 heaping tablespoon nigella seeds or toasted sesame seeds

I. Bring a medium pot of salted water to a boil over high heat and add the fennel. As soon as the water begins to boil, blanch the fennel for 2 minutes. Remove and drain in a colander.

2. Whisk together the olive oil, vinegar, orange juice, salt, and pepper. Combine the arugula and fennel in a mixing bowl, and toss with the dressing. Reserve 2 tablespoons of the dressing for drizzling on top of the salad.

3. Place the greens on a round platter. Cut the cheese slices into 4 equal pieces and place around the greens on the platter. Drizzle the remaining dressing over the cheese. Sprinkle with the nigella or sesame seeds and serve.

Warm Fried Spinach Salad with Orange and Garlic

In the Mani, in the southern Peloponnisos, oranges flavor everything from the local olives and cured pork and sausages to this simple yet elegant spinach dish. Serve it with rustic panfried or grilled sausages, with grilled chicken kebabs, and with grilled fish simply seasoned with a little olive oil, lemon juice, and salt.

MAKES 4 TO 6 SERVINGS

$1\frac{1}{2}$ pounds fresh flat-leaf spinach

1 large navel orange

$\frac{2}{3}$ cup extra virgin olive oil

2 garlic cloves, thinly sliced

Salt to taste

I. Wash and spin dry the spinach. Using a sharp paring knife, cut the rind of the orange into 1-inch strips, getting some of the pith and fruit as you go.

2. Heat the olive oil in a large, deep skillet. Add the spinach. As soon as the spinach wilts, add the garlic, season with salt, and add the slices of orange rind. Cover the skillet, lower the heat to medium-low, and cook the spinach for about 20 minutes until dark and completely soft. Serve warm in a deep dish or bowl, together with the cooking juices, garlic, and rind.

Warm Potato Salad with Tomatoes, Onion, and Oregano

The herb that seasons so many Greek dishes is oregano, which grows wild all over the country. This salad, a local specialty from the island of lkaria, is usually served warm and meant to be filling. Some people add cut-up boiled eggs to it. Pungent red onions are a must.

MAKES 6 TO 8 SERVINGS

1 pound waxy potatoes (about 4)

2 medium tomatoes

1 large hothouse cucumber, peeled, halved lengthwise, and cut into $\frac{1}{4}$-inch slices

1 large red onion, coarsely chopped

2 hard-boiled eggs, peeled and quartered (optional)

$\frac{1}{3}$ to $\frac{1}{2}$ cup extra virgin Greek olive oil to taste

3 to 4 tablespoons red wine vinegar to taste

Salt and freshly ground black pepper to taste

3 tablespoons fresh oregano leaves or 1 teaspoon dried Greek oregano

I. Rinse and scrub the potatoes. Do not peel. Bring them to a boil over high heat in a large pot of lightly salted water. Reduce the heat and simmer until the skins begin to burst open and the flesh is tender, or 30 to 35 minutes. Remove, drain, and set aside until cool enough to handle.

2. Peel the potatoes when they are still warm and cut into quarters or sixths. Place in a serving bowl. Cut the tomatoes into 1-inch cubes and add to the potatoes. Add the cucumbers and onion. Place the eggs, if using, around the top of the salad. Pour in the olive oil and vinegar, season with salt, pepper, and oregano, toss gently, and serve immediately.

Beet and Feta Cheese Salad

At tavernas all over Greece people will take a little wedge of feta and mash it up in their plates, then pick up a piece of beet salad with the same fork, a combination that both looks and tastes great together. This is a decidedly more refined version of that rustic combination.

MAKES 6 TO 8 SERVINGS

3 large beets, trimmed and scrubbed

FOR THE DRESSING

1½ cups liquid from the cooked beets, strained

⅓ cup dark brown sugar

3 allspice berries

Salt

2 to 4 tablespoons balsamic vinegar to taste

½ pound Greek feta, coarsely crumbled

2 Belgian endives, leaves separated

4 to 6 tablespoons extra virgin olive oil to taste

Freshly ground black pepper

Fresh mint leaves

I. Place the beets in a medium saucepan filled three-quarters of the way up with water, and bring to a boil over high heat. Reduce the heat and simmer until the beets are tender. Strain and reserve the liquid. Let the beets cool.

2. Bring the beet liquid to a boil in a small saucepan. Add the sugar, allspice berries, and a little salt. Reduce the heat and simmer, uncovered, until reduced by half. Taste and adjust seasoning with the vinegar. Simmer another 5 minutes or so until the mixture is syrupy. You must be careful not to leave the liquid unattended on the stove. It will seem like nothing is happening for ages, and then all of a sudden the sugar will caramelize. When it does, and the sauce thickens, remove immediately.

3. While the dressing is simmering, peel the beets and cut them into ¼-inch dice. Combine with the feta, tossing gently. Place 2 heaping tablespoons of the mixture inside the endive leaves and place decoratively on a serving platter. Drizzle with olive oil to taste, then drizzle with the dressing. Do not drench with either. Season with pepper, garnish with mint, and serve.

White Bean Salad with Peppers, Onion, and Anchovies

This lovely, robust salad is an embellished version of a well-known meze called *piaz*, from Thessaloniki.

MAKES 6 TO 8 SERVINGS

6 ounces dried white canellini or navy beans, soaked overnight

2 tablespoons extra virgin Greek olive oil for sautéing,
plus 1/3 cup for the dressing

1 medium red onion, finely chopped

1 cup (about 3) seeded and finely chopped
Italian frying peppers

2 garlic cloves, finely chopped

3 salted anchovies

2 heaping tablespoons snipped dill

Juice of 1 large lemon

Salt to taste

Cayenne pepper to taste

Paprika to taste

I. Drain the beans. Bring to a boil over medium heat in ample fresh cold water. Lower the heat and simmer the beans for about 1 hour, or until tender but not disintegrating. About 10 minutes before the beans are done, season them with salt. Remove, drain, and rinse in a colander under cold water. Place in a serving bowl.

2. Heat the 2 tablespoons olive oil in a large skillet and sauté the onion, peppers, and garlic over medium heat for about 5 minutes, or until the mixture begins to get translucent. In the meanwhile, rinse the anchovies very well and mince. Add the anchovies to the skillet and stir together with the vegetable mixture for another 3 to 4 minutes. Remove from the heat.

3. Add the sautéed vegetables to the beans. Toss lightly to combine. Add the remaining ingredients and mix well. Cover and let the beans sit for 1 hour at room temperature before serving. You can also make this dish several hours ahead of time, in which case you should store the bean salad, covered, in the refrigerator. Bring it to room temperature before serving.

Lentil-Bulgur Salad with Parsley and Hot Peppers

Lentils and bulgur wheat are two of the oldest ingredients in the Greek pantry. This salad is both filling and refreshing, with a little bit of a bite from the hot peppers. There are many varieties of lentils; look for small or baby green lentils, which are less starchy and work best in this dish.

MAKES 6 TO 8 SERVINGS

1 cup coarse bulgur

2 cups cold water

$1\frac{1}{2}$ cups small green lentils

1 bay leaf

2 cups finely chopped fresh flat-leaf parsley

2 large tomatoes, seeded and diced

4 scallions, finely chopped

1 garlic clove, finely chopped

1 to 2 fresh chile peppers to taste, seeded and finely chopped

$\frac{1}{2}$ teaspoon ground cinnamon

$\frac{1}{2}$ teaspoon ground cumin

$\frac{1}{2}$ cup extra virgin olive oil

Juice of 1 lemon

Salt to taste

I. Soak the bulgur in a large bowl with the cold water. Leave it for about 2 hours, or until it absorbs all the water.

2. Rinse the lentils under the tap in a colander and pick through them for small pebbles. Place in a saucepan with enough water to cover by 2 inches. Place the bay leaf in the pot. Bring to a boil, reduce the heat to low, and simmer until tender but al dente. Remove, drain, and rinse in a colander under cold water. Discard the bay leaf.

3. In a large mixing bowl, combine the lentils and bulgur. Mix in the parsley, tomatoes, scallions, garlic, chile peppers, and spices. Toss with the olive oil and lemon juice, and season with salt. Refrigerate, covered, for 1 hour before serving.

Fresh Fava Bean and Octopus Salad

Seafood and beans are a classic Mediterranean combination. This salad is lovely, hearty, and enticing.

1 medium octopus, about 2 pounds

½ cup olive oil

1 large bay leaf

2 garlic cloves

1 lemon, halved

1 small orange, halved

2 pounds large fresh fava beans, shelled

4 scallions

1 large tomato, peeled

1 large garlic clove, minced

Sea salt and freshly ground black pepper to taste

1 tablespoon chopped fresh tarragon
or 1 scant teaspoon dried tarragon

FOR THE DRESSING

½ cup extra virgin olive oil

Juice of 1 lemon

½ cup octopus cooking juices

I. Wash and clean the octopus: Cut it just below the eyes, removing and discarding its hood, and then squeezing out its little beak. Place the octopus in a large, heavy pot with the olive oil, bay leaf, and garlic. Squeeze the lemon and orange juices into the pot, over the octopus. Cover and heat over very low flame for about 50 minutes, or until the octopus has exuded its own juices and has turned deep pink and tender. Remove. Strain and reserve the pan juices. Let the octopus cool slightly, then cut it into ¼-inch-thick slices.

2. While the octopus is cooking, wash and drain the beans. Bring a large pot of water to a boil and blanch the beans for about 10 minutes, until tender but al dente. Drain in a colander (see Note).

3. Trim the scallions, using only the whites and most tender parts of the greens, and cut into thin rounds. Cut the tomato in half, gently squeeze out the seeds, and dice into ¼-inch cubes.

4. Combine the beans, octopus, scallions, garlic, and tomato in a serving bowl. Season with salt, pepper, and tarragon. Toss very gently. Whisk together the olive oil, lemon juice, and ½ cup of the octopus pan juices until smooth. Pour this over the salad, season to taste with salt and pepper, toss again, and serve immediately.

NOTE

Most Greek cooks do not peel fresh favas. The young beans are tender as they are. If you prefer them skinned, however, just peel away the outer layer with a paring knife after they are blanched, drained, and cool enough to handle.

VARIATION

You can replace the fava beans with navy or canellini beans. Use 1¹/₂ cups beans, soaked overnight, then cooked until tender.

Greek Tuna Salad with Wild Herbs and Onions

In the annals of Greek restaurant history, especially the long chapter on immigrant livelihoods in America, the diner holds a loving place. I spent many a Friday night of my youth cruising the streets of Queens, then stopping for a late snack at one of the avatars of *haute* teen cuisine, the local diner. The tuna salad came served from an ice cream scoop on a leaf of iceberg lettuce. When you're seventeen, that's chic.

Tuna salad made its way from the diners of America to the menus of returning Greek immigrants, many of whom entered the restaurant business in their homeland, too. For a time, and to this day, Greek tuna salad consisted of a plate full of canned tuna mixed with carrots and celery and topped with a sheath of glistening mayonnaise. This version is a decidedly more aromatic, refined version of a dish that, to me, recalls the rapacious appetites of adolescence. If it means anything my own daughter, not quite a teenager at this writing, loves it. It's her dad's recipe.

MAKES 4 TO 6 SERVINGS

3 cups good-quality canned tuna, preserved in water or olive oil

3 scallions, finely chopped

1 medium carrot, finely chopped

1 celery stalk, finely chopped

1 medium fennel bulb, finely chopped

3 tablespoons small capers, rinsed and drained

$\frac{1}{3}$ cup finely chopped wild fennel or fennel fronds

$\frac{1}{2}$ cup finely chopped fresh dill

6 tablespoons extra virgin olive oil

Juice of 1 small lemon

Salt to taste

1 scant teaspoon paprika

1 lemon, sliced into thin rounds

1. Rinse and drain the tuna. Combine the tuna, scallions, carrot, celery, fennel, capers, and herbs.

2. Toss with the olive oil and lemon juice and season with salt. Place in a medium serving bowl, sprinkle with paprika, garnish with lemon slices around the rim, and serve.

Warm Chicken Salad with Tarator Sauce

Chicken is something Greeks usually grill, stuff, or roast. Chicken salad is a novel concept, but this salad makes good use of leftover chicken and couples it with an enriched version of a classic Anatolian Greek sauce.

6 to 8 tablespoons extra virgin olive oil to taste

2 celery stalks, finely chopped

2 scallions, finely chopped

3 cups cooked, shredded chicken

2/3 cup walnuts

4 large garlic cloves, minced

3 cups chopped fresh spinach leaves

2 to 3 tablespoons red wine vinegar to taste

1 1/2 cups thick Greek or Mediterranean-style yogurt or drained plain yogurt (see Note)

Salt and freshly ground black pepper to taste

Paprika and parsley leaves for garnish

3 heads Belgian endive (optional)

I. Heat 2 tablespoons of the olive oil in a skillet and cook the celery and scallions for a few minutes until pearly and softened. Add the chicken and stir to warm through. Set aside, covered, in a low oven to keep warm.

2. Place the walnuts and garlic in the bowl of a food processor, and pulse on and off until mealy. Add the chopped spinach and pulse on and off, drizzling in 3 tablespoons olive oil and 2 tablespoons of the vinegar in alternating doses as you do this. The mixture should be moist.

3. Heat 1 more tablespoon of olive oil over very low heat in a nonstick skillet and spoon in the walnut-spinach mixture. Gently fold in the yogurt, stirring continually, and add 1 or 2 tablespoons more of olive oil. As soon as the mixture is warmed through, remove.

Toss with the chicken-celery mixture, salt, and pepper. Adjust the seasoning with additional olive oil or vinegar. Spread or mound on a serving plate or in a bowl, sprinkled with a little paprika and parsley leaves for color. You may also serve this in individual portions, spooned into Belgian endive leaves if desired. Drizzle a little olive oil over each portion and sprinkle with paprika and parsley.

NOTE

You can find already drained, very thick and creamy Greek or Mediterranean-style yogurt in specialty shops across the United States, or you can drain your own: Start with double the quantity that you will need, place it in a colander lined with a double cheesecloth, and drain for 2 to 3 hours until as thick as sour cream.

SMALL EGG DISHES

Egg cookery in Greece is shamelessly rich and refreshingly devoid of any concern over the C-words, cholesterol and calories.

I have no qualms about frying up thin slivers of potatoes in olive oil, adding a grated tomato, breaking two eggs over them, topping them with feta just as the whites congeal, then serving up the whole thing with a salad, a few olives, bread, of course, and a glass of crisp, white Greek wine or even ouzo, which matches such a heady combination of flavors perfectly. That would be a dish in the spirit of ad hoc mezethes, not refined, not pretentious, and certainly meant to be indulged in with gusto if a few friends happen to drop in and there happens to be not very much on hand to offer them.

Other egg dishes require more planning.

Omelets, for example, are favorite quick and savory dishes on meze menus, and there are many regional variations. They all basically follow the same tenets: Sauté the vegetables in a large skillet in ample olive oil until soft, lightly beat the desired number of eggs, pour them over the vegetables, tilt, and serve when the eggs are set. Greek omelets are rustic. They are usually large, round, pielike creations cooked over the whole skillet, rarely filled, folded, and flipped. Some are baked. They are cut into wedges from the center out and served like slices of pizza. I have included three omelets in the batch of recipes that follow. Favored vegetables to be concealed under the cover of eggs in a skillet are artichokes, wild asparagus, zucchini, onions, and tomatoes. Greeks make omelets with greens, too. Spinach and chard are two favorites.

Hard-boiled eggs, eggs baked in embers, stuffed eggs, and vegetables stuffed with eggs make up the rest of the gamut of egg cookery in Greece, not including, of course, the famed avgolemono (egg-lemon), a velvety liaison that can be both sauce and soup, depending on how thick you make it. Perhaps the one thing that distinguishes egg cookery more than anything else in Greece is that eggs are savored less for breakfast and more as a quick and easy lunch, dinner, or snack.

Hard-Boiled Eggs Stuffed with Tomato, Onion, and Olive Oil

The filling for this easy dish comes from a Greek island dip that calls for nothing but good tomato paste, olive oil, and onions.

MAKES 6 TO 12 SERVINGS

6 large eggs, hard boiled

$\frac{1}{2}$ cup good-quality, preferably organic, tomato paste

$\frac{1}{3}$ cup extra virgin olive oil

1 small red onion, finely chopped

Salt and pepper

I. Peel and halve the eggs. Scoop out the yolks and mash with a fork.

2. In a small bowl, mix together the tomato paste, mashed egg yolks, olive oil, and onion. Season with salt and pepper, and spoon or pipe back into the hollowed-out whites. Serve.

Open-Faced Cauliflower Omelet with Shaved Botargo and Black Pepper

This is a recipe born in the region of my own kitchen. I absolutely adore the combination of cauliflower, pepper, and botargo, the pressed, preserved roe of the gray mullet, which is considered one of the most expensive delicacies in the Aegean. In Greece, botargo comes from the natural fisheries along the western coast, from the northern side of the Peloponnese all the way up to Preveza, and along some of the nearby islands, such as Lefkada. The season for producing it is October, when the mullets spawn. The roe is removed whole in its sacs, salted, and dried outdoors. When it has reached the desired density, producers hand-dip it in beeswax to preserve it.

MAKES 10 TO 12 SERVINGS

2 tablespoons unsalted butter

2 tablespoons extra virgin olive oil

$\frac{1}{2}$ cup finely chopped scallion whites

1 garlic clove, minced

2 cups finely cut cauliflower florets

5 eggs

4 tablespoons heavy cream

Salt and freshly ground white pepper to taste

One 2-inch piece of botargo, cleaned and sliced paper thin

Juice of $\frac{1}{2}$ lemon

Cracked black peppercorns to taste

I. In a 10- or 12-inch nonstick skillet, heat the butter and olive oil and sauté the scallions and garlic over medium-high heat for about 5 minutes, stirring. Add the cauliflower florets and continue cooking over medium heat until they are tender and lightly browned, about 20 minutes. Stir frequently while they cook.

2. Meanwhile, break 3 of the eggs into a bowl. Separate the yolks and whites from the remaining 2 eggs and add the yolks to the eggs in the bowl. Lightly beat, drizzling in the cream as you go. Using a wire whisk or electric mixer, whip the whites until soft peaks form. Fold the whites into the egg-and-cream mixture.

3. Pour this over the cauliflower in the skillet, tilting so that the egg goes all over and covers the entire surface of the pan. Reduce the heat, cover, and cook over low heat until the bottom is a pale gold and set. Take a plate, place it over the surface of the pan, and flip the omelet. Slip it back into the pan to cook a little on the other side. Remove to a platter. Sprinkle the shaved botargo over the top of the omelet and season with a little lemon juice and black pepper. Cut into 10 or 12 equal pie-shaped wedges and serve immediately.

Chard, Tomato, and Feta Cheese Omelet

This is one of many Greek omelets that call for greens. Serve this with Greek Fries (page 98), wrinkled black olives, and crisp white wine or retsina.

MAKES 8 SERVINGS

4 cups coarsely chopped chard or spinach

3 tablespoons extra virgin Greek olive oil

1 medium red onion, finely chopped

2 tablespoons good-quality tomato paste

1½ cups (about 6 ounces) crumbled Greek feta

5 large eggs, lightly beaten

Salt and freshly ground black pepper

I. Wash and drain the chard very well. Heat the olive oil over medium heat in a 10- or 12-inch nonstick skillet. Add the onion, reduce the heat to low, and cook, stirring, until the onion is wilted and lightly golden, or 12 to 15 minutes. Add the tomato paste and stir. Add the chard or spinach and season with salt and pepper. Raise the heat to medium, stir all the ingredients together, and cook until the chard is wilted and all of the pan juices have cooked off.

2. Add the feta and stir until it has nearly melted, or 5 to 7 minutes.

3. Beat the eggs with a little salt and pepper. Add them to the skillet and tilt it so that the eggs go all over, covering the entire surface of the pan. Do this several times as they cook, so that the omelet is dry and fluffy and not at all runny. Adjust the seasoning with additional salt and pepper and serve warm or at room temperature.

Spicy Sausage in a Skillet with Tomatoes, Peppers, Eggs, and Cheese

In the meze emporiums of Thessaloniki, where so many Anatolian Greeks settled, this is popular fare, the kind of dish you might even order two servings of and some extra bread to go with it.

MAKES 4 TO 6 SERVINGS

3 tablespoons extra virgin olive oil

2 tablespoons good-quality tomato paste

2 medium green bell peppers, seeded and chopped

1 cup chopped, peeled plum tomatoes, drained of their juices

One 8- or 10-inch spicy air-dried sausage, preferably Armenian soutzouki, cut into 1/4-inch rounds

Salt and freshly ground black pepper to taste

2 to 4 eggs, slightly beaten, as needed

1/2 cup (about 2 ounces) coarsely grated Kasseri cheese or Gouda

I. Heat the olive oil and tomato paste together over low heat in a large skillet. Add the peppers and cook until soft, or 8 to 10 minutes. Stir frequently as you cook them.

2. Add the tomatoes. As soon as they come to a boil, add the sausage. Season with salt and pepper, reduce the heat, cover, and cook for 5 to 8 minutes, or until the mixture is thick. Add the eggs, stir lightly to scramble in the pan, and cook until set but not dry.

3. Sprinkle in the grated cheese, heat for a minute or so longer, and as soon as it begins to melt, serve.

Sunny-Side-Up Eggs Cooked over Spicy Vegetables

This is a wonderful, easy summer meze that goes very well with chilled retsina.

2 tablespoons extra virgin olive oil

1 tablespoon unsalted butter

1 large red onion, finely chopped

1 green bell pepper, seeded and finely chopped

1 hot green pepper, seeded and finely chopped

2 large tomatoes, peeled, seeded, and grated
(see Note on page 171) or finely chopped

Salt and freshly ground black pepper to taste

4 small eggs

1/2 teaspoon sweet or hot paprika

2 to 3 tablespoons thick Greek yogurt or sour cream to taste

I. Heat the olive oil and butter over medium heat in a 10-inch nonstick skillet. Add the onion and peppers, and cook until soft, or about 10 minutes.

2. Add the tomatoes. Season with salt and pepper, and simmer over low heat, covered, until the sauce has thickened, or 10 to 15 minutes.

3. Uncover the skillet and carefully break the eggs over the vegetable mixture. Cook over low heat, uncovered, until the eggs are set. Season to taste with additional salt and pepper, and serve. Sprinkle if desired with a little sweet or hot paprika, and serve with a dollop of yogurt or sour cream.

Mushrooms Stuffed with Asparagus and Eggs

In Greece connoisseurs of the wild side of life take to the countryside in early spring to stalk the thin, sweet strands of asparagus that grow untamed in many parts of the country. Wild asparagus is one of the best things to reap from the rich Greek flora, tender, refreshing as dew, delicate. It is also one of the favorite ingredients to match up with eggs, usually in the form of an omelet. That said, it is virtually impossible to find wild asparagus in the U.S., unless one follows the Greek example and forages for it when it sprouts each March, April, and May. I have taken the idea of an asparagus omelet, married it with mushrooms, and altered the wild ingredient in favor of cultivated asparagus.

MAKES 8 TO 16 SERVINGS

4 asparagus stalks, trimmed

8 large portobello mushrooms, about 4 inches in diameter

4 tablespoons extra virgin olive oil, plus more for brushing the pan

4 scallions, finely chopped (whites and as much of the greens as possible)

4 garlic cloves, finely chopped

Salt and freshly ground black pepper to taste

3 eggs

3 tablespoons heavy cream

1¼ cups crumbled Greek feta

I. Cut the asparagus into small pieces, about 1 inch long. Bring a medium saucepan of salted water to a rolling boil and blanch the asparagus until tender, 5 to 7 minutes. Remove and drain immediately in a colander.

2. Remove the stems from the mushrooms and chop them. Place the chopped mushroom stems in a food processor and pulse on and off until they are minced fine.

3. Heat 2 tablespoons of the olive oil over medium heat in a medium skillet and cook the scallions until wilted. Add the garlic and stir. Add the mushroom stems, season with salt and pepper, and sauté until the liquid they exude cooks off. Using a teaspoon, carefully scrape and discard the black ruffled interior of each mushroom cap. Be careful not to tear or break the caps.

4. Preheat the oven to 350°F. Lightly oil an ovenproof glass baking dish large enough to fit the mushrooms.

5. Break the eggs into a bowl, and lightly beat with a fork. Add the cream and beat a little more to combine. Place the egg mixture, mushroom mixture, and feta in a mixing bowl, and stir to combine. Place the mushroom caps in the baking pan. Brush with the remaining olive oil and season lightly with salt. Spoon several tablespoons of the filling into each cap, leaving a little room at the top for the egg to expand while baking. Take a few pieces of asparagus and place them in each cap, tucking them slightly down with your finger. Season with pepper.

6. Cover the pan with aluminum foil and bake in the middle of the oven for 35 to 40 minutes, or until the eggs are set and the mushrooms tender. Cool slightly and serve. The stuffed mushrooms may also be served at room temperature.

PHYLLO PIES IN PANS AND HANDS

Years ago, when I first saw Greek spinach triangles in the frozen food section of a big suburban supermarket, I knew that Greek cuisine finally had come mainstream. That the favorite food of my childhood, prepared by an orchestra of loving female hands on every holiday, could now be had in a moment's notice by popping a tray into the microwave seemed somehow to dilute the memory for me. I was secretly glad to note that the commercial stuff tastes nothing like the savory pies I remember as a girl. I still get tremendous pleasure from making these and other pastries, and even more pleasure from serving them. Greek pies are the ultimate meze food.

Like all wrapped foods, the savory pies appeal to our desire for surprise and discovery. They contain an element of fun, which is inherent in the whole meze experience. They satisfy the need for variety—each bite opens up a range of flavors and textures, at once contrasting and complementing each other.

The pie recipes in this book are purposefully easy. All of them call for commercial phyllo as opposed to more complicated and time-consuming homemade pastry.

WORKING WITH PHYLLO

The recipes in this chapter call for either standard #4 frozen phyllo, which is slightly thicker than #7 and better suited for dense savory fillings; for frozen puff pastry, which is sold either rolled in sheets (two to a pack) or in individual 4-inch circular pieces, or for Turkish yufka, which I recommend in two of the bite-sized pie recipes. Yufka is available via mail order (see page 192) and may also be found in Middle Eastern markets.

In a standard 1-pound box of frozen #4 phyllo, there are usually about 18 sheets. If there are one or two fewer or more, it doesn't make much of a difference. Recipes can be adjusted a little. For recipes that require fewer than 18 sheets, you can reroll the leftovers, cover, and enclose them in a large Ziploc bag in the refrigerator for a few days. Defrosted phyllo cannot be refrozen.

Opening a box of phyllo is a little like buying a pig in a blanket. You never quite know what you are going to get. That's why it is important to buy frozen phyllo from shops with heavy volume—it's one way to ensure that the supplies are always fresh.

Phyllo should be frozen properly. If the sheets have somehow gotten wet, the moisture will crystallize and cause the pastry to stick together or become soggy. Phyllo that is brittle is usually past its prime. Neither problem means that you should throw away the entire pack. Once the phyllo bakes or is fried, tears and other irregularities won't show. The soggy or brittle parts can often be trimmed off.

All phyllo needs to be properly defrosted, overnight from the freezer to the fridge and then for several hours at room temperature. It should always be at room temperature when working with it, to ensure that it is pliant and not brittle.

BAKING VS. FRYING

Many traditional meze recipes, especially for individual pieces such as triangles or rolls, call for the pieces to be fried rather than baked on sheet pans. Most are suitable for both cooking methods. Baking is obviously lighter, and brushing the surface of each pastry with olive oil or melted butter will result in a crisp, delicate final texture. If you opt for the skillet, make sure the individual pieces are sealed along the seam. Brushing the edges with water or egg white will secure them closed. Drain them on paper towels before serving.

STORAGE

With the exception of the open-faced pies and the seafood pie, all the dishes in this chapter may be made right up through the final step before baking or frying. At that point, they can be covered and frozen, preferably on sheet pans, and baked or fried directly from the freezer.

Add the sugar and continue cooking over low heat for another 10 minutes or so, or until the mixture is lightly caramelized. Remove and cool slightly.

3. Combine the cheeses in a large mixing bowl. Add the dried tomatoes, fresh tomatoes, onion-garlic mixture, and spices. Pour in the remaining olive oil and combine. Taste and adjust with salt.

4. Preheat the oven to 350°F. Lightly oil a sheet pan. While you work, keep the phyllo covered with a kitchen towel, and cover that one with another, damp, kitchen towel. Remove the first sheet, and place it horizontally on your work surface. Brush lightly with olive oil. Place a second sheet on top and brush that with olive oil, too. Spread about 3 tablespoons of the filling across the bottom width of the pastry, about 1 inch from the edge. Fold the bottom edge and sides over the filling, then roll it up to form a cylinder. Roll the phyllo inward from one end to form a coil. Place seam side down on the sheet pan. Cover with a kitchen towel as you continue with the remaining phyllo and filling. Place the twists about 1 inch apart on the sheet pan. When they are all formed, sprinkle the tops with a little cold water. Bake for 20 to 25 minutes, or until lightly golden and crisp. Remove, cool slightly, and serve.

Pumpkin-Cheese Triangles

Pumpkin comes to market in the late fall in Greece, and then is cooked in dozens of meze recipes. I love it sliced into wedges, floured and fried, then served with a dollop of garlicky skordalia, or in fritters, bursting with mint and onions, which is how pumpkin is savored in our native village on Ikaria. Pumpkin pies abound, though, in both savory and sweet versions, and here I have combined the main ingredients of Ikarian fritters and enclosed them in golden phyllo.

MAKES ABOUT 36 TRIANGLES

FOR THE FILLING

1½ pounds pumpkin, peeled and seeded

½ cup (about 2 ounces) grated aged Greek myzithra cheese or pecorino Romano

½ cup fresh Greek myzithra cheese or whole-milk ricotta (about ¼ pound)

½ cup chopped fresh dill leaves

½ cup chopped fresh mint leaves

1 teaspoon anise seeds, ground

1 large egg, lightly beaten

Salt and freshly ground black pepper to taste

1 pound (about 18 sheets) commercial phyllo, defrosted and at room temperature

Olive oil for brushing pastry

I. Make the filling: Grate the pumpkin. Place in a colander with a little salt and knead. Let the pumpkin drain in the colander for 1 hour. Squeeze between the palms of your hands to rid it of as much liquid as possible. Place in a bowl and combine with the grated myzithra or pecorino, the fresh myzithra or ricotta, dill, mint, and anise seeds. Mix in the egg and season with salt and pepper.

2. Preheat the oven to 350°F. Lightly oil 2 baking sheets. Place the phyllo in a stack in front of you on your work surface. Cut into 4 equal columns, stack, and cover with one dry kitchen towel and one damp one.

3. Take the first strip of phyllo and brush lightly with olive oil. Cover with a second strip and brush that with oil. Place 1 teaspoon of the filling on the bottom right corner of the phyllo, leaving some space along the edge. Fold up the right-hand corner to form a right triangle and continue folding up from corner to corner, as though folding a flag. Place seam side down on the baking sheet. Cover with a kitchen towel as you continue with the remaining filling and phyllo. Place the triangles about 1 inch apart and brush the tops lightly with olive oil. Bake in the center of the oven until lightly golden, or 12 to 15 minutes. Remove, cool slightly, and serve.

Spinach and Three-Cheese Triangles

Little spinach-cheese triangles are probably among the most familiar Greek party foods. This recipe is enriched with several kinds of cheese and fresh herbs.

MAKES ABOUT 36 TRIANGLES

4 tablespoons extra-virgin olive oil,
  plus more for brushing pastry

2 cups chopped, blanched, drained spinach
  (about 6 cups fresh, or 1 pound frozen and defrosted)

1/2 cup chopped fresh mint

1/2 cup chopped fresh flat-leaf parsley

Salt and freshly ground black pepper to taste

1/3 cup ouzo

1 cup (about 4 ounces) crumbled feta

1 cup (about 4 ounces) crumbled Greek manouri cheese
  or ricotta salata

1/2 cup (about 4 ounces) fresh anthotyro, whole-milk ricotta,
  or farmer's cheese

1 large egg, slightly beaten

1 pound (about 18 sheets) commercial phyllo,
  defrosted and at room temperature

Olive or other vegetable oil for frying, as needed

I. Heat 2 tablespoons of the olive oil in a large heavy skillet over medium heat and sauté the spinach and herbs for a few minutes until all their liquid has cooked off. Season with salt and pepper. Pour in the ouzo and as soon as it boils off, remove the mixture from the heat. Set aside to cool a little.

2. Combine the spinach and herb mixture with the cheeses in a large bowl. Add the egg and the remaining 2 tablespoons of olive oil. Adjust the seasoning with additional salt and pepper.

3. Preheat the oven to 350°F. Brush a sheet pan with oil, then line it with parchment paper. Place the phyllo vertically in front of you on your work surface. Using a sharp knife, cut lengthwise into 4 equal columns. Stack and cover with a dry kitchen towel and immediately on top of that place a damp kitchen towel.

4. Remove the first phyllo sheet and place it vertically in front of you. Brush lightly with olive oil. Place another sheet on top and brush that lightly, too. Place a teaspoon of the filling on the bottom right-hand corner of the phyllo and fold up like a flag in order to form a small triangle. Place on the baking sheet seam side down. Cover with a kitchen towel as you continue with the remaining filling and phyllo. Brush all the triangles with olive oil. Bake for about 15 minutes, or until the triangles are lightly golden and puffy. Remove and serve.

VARIATION

The triangles may also be fried. Seal the seam of each triangle closed by brushing with a little water. Heat 2 inches of olive or other vegetable oil in a large skillet and fry the triangles a few at a time. Remove when golden, drain on paper towels, and serve.

Macedonian Paprika–Onion Phyllo Triangles

MAKES 24 TRIANGLES

⅓ cup extra virgin Greek olive oil,
  plus more for brushing pastries

6 large red onions, sliced (about 10 cups)

1 tablespoon sweet Hungarian paprika

Pinch of nutmeg

Salt and freshly ground white pepper to taste

12 sheets commercial phyllo, defrosted
  and at room temperature

1 cup thick Greek or Mediterranean-style yogurt or
  drained plain yogurt (see Note on page 51)

I. Heat the olive oil in a large, preferably nonstick, skillet and cook the onions over low heat, stirring frequently, until golden, about 20 minutes. Add the paprika, nutmeg, salt, and pepper, and continue cooking until the mixture is very soft and deep red. Remove and cool slightly.

2. Preheat the oven to 350°F. Lightly oil 2 baking sheets.

3. Have the phyllo ready. Place the sheets in front of you and, using a sharp knife, cut lengthwise into 4 equally wide columns. Stack them, and keep the stack covered with a dry kitchen towel and then over that a damp kitchen towel.

4. Remove 1 strip of phyllo, brush it lightly with olive oil, and place another strip on top. Brush that with oil, too. Place a teaspoon or so of the filling in the lower right-hand corner of the phyllo, about ½ inch from the edge. Fold up the right corner to form a right triangle, and continue folding, the way one folds a flag. Place seam side down on the baking sheet. Cover with a kitchen towel and continue until the phyllo and filling are used up. Brush the tops of the triangles lightly with olive oil. Bake in the center of the oven for about 15 minutes, or until puffed and golden. Serve warm, two to a plate, with a little dollop of yogurt on the side.

Three-Cheese Phyllo Triangles with Onions and Yogurt

Onion, cheese, and yogurt pies abound in the north of Greece, especially in shepherds' communities where dairy products are daily staples. This recipe is culled from that tradition, but instead of preparing a whole sheet pan with homemade phyllo, I have reworked it to make it accessible and more in tune with the meze style of eating.

MAKES ABOUT 36 TRIANGLES

FOR THE FILLING

1/3 cup extra virgin olive oil, plus more for brushing pastries

2 large onions, finely chopped (about 2 cups)

1 1/2 cups (about 12 ounces) fresh Greek myzithra, whole-milk ricotta, or farmer's cheese, crumbled

3/4 cup (about 3 ounces) Greek feta, crumbled

3/4 cup (about 2 ounces) grated Greek kefalotyri cheese or other hard sheep's milk cheese, such as pecorino

1/2 cup thick Greek or Mediterranean-style yogurt or drained plain yogurt (see Note on page 51)

1/3 cup finely chopped fresh dill

2 large eggs

Salt and freshly ground black pepper to taste

1 pound (about 18 sheets) commercial phyllo, defrosted and at room temperature

I. Heat 3 tablespoons of the olive oil over medium heat in a large, preferably nonstick, skillet and cook the onions until soft and lightly golden, or 10 to 12 minutes. Stir as you cook them. Remove from the heat and set aside.

2. Combine the cheeses, yogurt, remaining olive oil, cooked onions, and dill. Beat the eggs lightly and add to the mixture, mixing well. Season with salt and pepper.

3. Have the phyllo ready. Place the sheets in front of you and, using a sharp knife, cut length-wise into 4 equal columns. Stack them, and keep the stack covered with a dry kitchen towel and then over that a damp kitchen towel. Preheat the oven to 350°F, and lightly oil 2 baking sheets.

4. Remove 1 strip of phyllo, brush it lightly with olive oil, and place another strip on top. Brush that with oil, too. Place a teaspoon of the filling in the lower right-hand corner of the phyllo, about $\frac{1}{2}$ inch from the edge. Fold up the right corner to form a right triangle, and continue folding, the way one folds a flag. Place seam side down on the baking sheet. Continue until the phyllo and filling are used up. Bake in the center of the oven for 12 to 15 minutes, or until puffed and golden. Serve warm.

Brigitte's Eggplant or Zucchini Crescents

A few years ago, I placed an ad in the local English-language newspaper in Greece for a recipe tester and found a godsend in Brigitte Fatsio as a result. She has since become a friend. Her husband, from the Princess Islands in the Bosphorus, has a slew of extended family and what seems like an endless number of great-cooking aunts who have shared their recipes with Brigitte over the years. This and the next one are among them. Both call for Turkish yufka, which is available in Middle Eastern shops across the U.S. Phyllo or frozen puff pastry can be substituted, but the springy, resilient texture of the yufka is really what makes these dishes so delicious.

MAKES 12 CRESCENTS

2 large eggplants (about 1¾ pounds total)

¼ cup extra virgin olive oil, plus more for brushing pastries

½ cup (about 2 ounces) grated kasseri cheese

½ cup (about 4 ounces) crumbled Greek feta

1 large egg

Salt and freshly ground black pepper to taste

One 12-inch piece of Turkish yufka dough

Olive or other vegetable oil for frying (optional)

I. Preheat the broiler. Puncture the eggplants in various places with a fork and place them on a rack over a baking sheet. Grill about 8 inches from the heat of the broiler, turning, until softened on all sides. Do not char them; this is a dish that calls for the scent of roasted, but not smoky, eggplant. Remove, cool, and peel off their skins. Cut the eggplants in half; remove and discard as many of the seeds as possible. Chop them coarsely and leave them to drain in a colander for about 20 minutes.

2. In a large bowl, using a fork, combine the chopped eggplants, olive oil, cheeses, and egg. Season with salt and pepper.

3. Place the yufka dough in front of you. Using a large, sharp knife, cut the yufka into quarters. Repeat two more times to get 12 equal triangular wedges. Preheat the oven to 350°F. Lightly oil a baking sheet.

4. Separate the dough pieces. Take a heaping tablespoon of the filling and place it on the bottom of the dough, at its widest section, about ½ inch from the edge. Roll up to form a little crescent. Place seam side down on the baking sheet. Repeat with the remaining ingredients, brush the pastries with a little olive oil, and bake for about 25 minutes, or until golden and puffed.

5. If frying, seal the edge of each pastry with a little water. Heat about 2 inches of oil in a large, heavy skillet and fry a few pieces of the pastries at a time. Remove, drain on paper towels, and serve.

VARIATIONS

You can use puff pastry in lieu of the Turkish yufka, and may easily use precut rounds of frozen puff pastry. Add a tablespoon of the filling to each piece, fold over to form half-moons, press the edges together, and bake. To substitute phyllo, take 12 sheets, defrosted and at room temperature, and cut them in half lengthwise to get 24 strips. Take 2 strips at a time, place the filling on the bottom center and fold up from side to side to form a triangle. Seal the edges with water and fry as above.

To make with zucchini: Wash, trim, and shred 3 large zucchini. Heat 2 tablespoons olive oil in a large, heavy skillet and sauté the zucchini until totally wilted and until all the pan juices have cooked off. Let the zucchini cool slightly, mix with the remaining ingredients in the filling, and bake or fry as above.

Spicy Open–Faced Ground Lamb Pies

3 tablespoons extra virgin olive oil

1 medium onion, finely chopped

1 fresh chile pepper, seeded and chopped

1 roasted red bell pepper, skin and seeds removed
  and finely chopped

$\frac{1}{4}$ pound ground lamb

Salt and freshly ground black pepper to taste

$\frac{1}{2}$ teaspoon cinnamon

1 teaspoon dried mint

$\frac{1}{2}$ teaspoon sugar

1 cup finely chopped fresh flat-leaf parsley

1 pound frozen puff pastry, defrosted and at room temperature

$\frac{1}{2}$ cup melted unsalted butter for brushing

2 medium red onions, cut into paper-thin rings

1 large lemon, cut into 8 wedges or thick slices

I. Heat the olive oil in a large, heavy skillet over medium heat and cook the onion until lightly golden, about 10 minutes. Stir frequently. Add the chile pepper and roasted red pepper; continue stirring for 2 to 3 minutes. Remove from the heat.

2. In a mixing bowl, combine the ground meat with the onion-pepper mixture. Season with salt and pepper. Add the cinnamon, mint, sugar, and $\frac{1}{2}$ cup of the parsley, and combine thoroughly.

3. Preheat the oven to 350°F. Lightly oil a baking sheet. Cut 2 puff-pastry sheets into 8 equal squares. Brush the pastry with melted butter. Spread $1\frac{1}{2}$ to 2 tablespoons of the filling on the pastry, leaving about an inch around the edges. Turn in the edges to form a rim that encloses the meat. Brush the rims with a little melted butter. Place the pies on the baking sheet and bake for about 25 minutes, or until the puff pastry is golden and crisp and the meat cooked. Remove and serve, either hot or at room temperature, garnished with the red onion rings, the remaining parsley, and lemon wedges.

Bourekia with Ground Beef, Bulgur, and Walnuts

My friend and inveterate recipe tester Brigitte Fatsio shared this family recipe with me. Like the eggplant crescents (page 78), this dish harkens back to her family's Anatolian roots and calls for using Turkish yufka instead of commercial phyllo dough.

MAKES 18 TO 20 PIECES

½ cup coarse bulgur wheat

1 cup water

½ pound lean ground beef

⅓ cup ground walnuts

½ cup chopped fresh flat-leaf parsley

1 large red onion, finely chopped (about 1½ cups)

Salt and freshly ground black pepper to taste

Two 12-inch round sheets of Turkish yufka dough, defrosted and at room temperature

2 large eggs

1 cup plain bread crumbs

Olive or other vegetable oil for frying

I. Soak the bulgur in the water until the liquid is absorbed, about 2 hours. Drain off any water that hasn't been absorbed by then.

2. In a mixing bowl, combine the bulgur, ground beef, and walnuts. Add the parsley, onion, and salt and pepper. The mixture should be fairly dry.

3. Cut each piece of the yufka from the center outward like a pie, to form 9 or 10 equal, almost triangular wedges each, 18 to 20 in total. Place a scant tablespoon of the filling on the widest part of the wedge. Fold in the right and left sides to cover the filling and roll up to form a crescent. Continue until the yufka and filling are used up. The pieces will look like mini-croissants. Let them stand, covered with a kitchen towel, for about 15 minutes.

4. Beat the eggs well and have the bread crumbs spread on a platter. Heat 2 inches of oil in a large, heavy skillet. Turn each boureki in the beaten egg and then roll it in the bread crumbs. Fry several pieces at a time in the hot oil for 3 to 4 minutes, or until golden. Turn the pieces once as you fry to color on all sides. Drain on paper towels and serve hot.

VARIATION

To substitute phyllo, take a 1-pound box (about 18 sheets), defrosted and at room temperature, and cut each sheet in half lengthwise to get 40 strips. Take 2 strips at a time, place the filling on the bottom center, and fold up from side to side as you would a flag to form a triangle. Seal the edges with water and fry as above.

Phyllo Rolls with Spicy Sausage, Peppers, and Kasseri Cheese

In Greece Sunday afternoons are often the time to get together for family-style lunches. We usually go out with friends and kids in tow to one of several favorite, casual dining spots. One is a small taverna in Glyfada called Sarai Palace, run by a Greek from Turkey. The owner is a great cook, and these little phyllo cigars filled with spicy sausage, peppers, and cheese are one of his many bite-sized delicacies. The recipe calls for Armenian sausage, a dark, aromatic beef sausage that is easy to find in Greek and Middle Eastern food shops all over the U.S., but any spicy dry sausage will do.

MAKES 24 PIECES

2 tablespoons extra virgin olive oil, plus 1/3 cup for brushing phyllo

1½ large green bell peppers, finely chopped

1 large red onion, finely chopped

1 garlic clove, minced

16 sheets commercial phyllo, defrosted and at room temperature

24 two-inch long strips (about 1¼ pounds) of kasseri cheese

24 two-inch long strips of Armenian soutzouki sausage or any dry spicy sausage

½ cup melted, clarified unsalted butter

Olive oil or other vegetable oil for frying

I. Heat 2 tablespoons olive oil in a large, heavy skillet over medium heat and cook the peppers, onion, and garlic until wilted, about 10 minutes. Stir frequently.

2. Preheat the oven to 350°F. Brush a sheet pan with oil, then line it with parchment paper. Place the phyllo vertically in front of you on your work surface. Cut vertically into 3-inch strips using a sharp knife. Stack and cover with a dry kitchen towel and immediately on top of that place a damp kitchen towel.

3. Combine the remaining olive oil and melted butter in a bowl. Remove the first phyllo sheet and place it vertically in front of you. Brush sparingly with the oil-butter mixture. Place another sheet on top and brush that lightly, too. On the bottom end of the phyllo, about ½ inch from the edge, spread about 1 heaping teaspoon of the pepper-onion mixture. Place the cheese on top and then the sausage. Fold up the bottom edge and fold in the sides, then roll it up to form a tight cylinder. Place seam side down on the baking pan. Continue with the remaining filling, cheese, and sausage until done. Brush the rolls with olive oil and bake for about 15 minutes, or until golden. Serve warm.

VARIATION

The cylinders may also be fried. Seal the seam of each roll closed by brushing with a little water. Heat 2 inches of olive or other vegetable oil in a large skillet and fry the rolls a few at a time. Remove when golden, drain on paper towels, and serve.

Pita Kaisarias

The best pita Kaisarias I ever had was in an Armenian kebab house called the Three Stars (Tria Asteria) in a neighborhood in Athens called Nea Smyrni (New Smyrna). This area is where many Greek and Armenian refugees settled after their exodus from Turkey in the 1920s. Pita Kaisarias—so named after an area in Turkey that was home to many Greeks and Armenians and that also was renowned for its pastourma—is one of the most compelling combinations on the meze table. It's made with doughy but thin homemade phyllo pastry; it oozes with melted cheese and tomatoes, and it is pungent with gossamer strips of pastourma.

Pastourma is never absent from the serious meze lover's table. It is cured beef seasoned with a dense, sticky spice rub whose main flavor ingredient is fenugreek. Fenugreek imparts an indescribable aroma. It is resinous, hence the sticky, moist quality of the rub, which most people remove before eating. Pastourma tastes earthy, sweet, and musklike.

Pastourma is made from several cuts of beef, but the best is always from the loin. You can find it in Greek and Middle Eastern food shops. Most of what is available in the U.S. is produced by an Armenian company in Canada.

This savory pie is delicious because it marries a trio of ingredients that go naturally well together. Kasseri is a mild cheese, pastourma is spicy, tomatoes are refreshing, and the phyllo adds texture—either crisp or soft depending on what you fancy.

Here I offer two versions, the first more traditional in its use of phyllo, albeit commercial, not homemade, and the second easy and fast—all you have to do is fill pocketed pita bread with the mixture and panfry it in a buttered skillet.

MAKES 10 TO 12 SERVINGS

7 sheets commercial phyllo, defrosted and at room temperature

½ cup melted unsalted butter

2 cups (about 6 ounces) grated kasseri cheese

2 medium tomatoes, thinly sliced

Salt and freshly ground black pepper

12 thin slices pastourma, sticky spice rub removed

I. Preheat the oven to 350°F. Lightly oil a 9 X 13 X 2-inch baking pan.

2. Layer 4 sheets of phyllo on the bottom of the pan, brushing each with 1 tablespoon of the melted butter.

3. Sprinkle one-third of the cheese over the surface of the phyllo, and spread half the tomato slices on top. Season with a little salt and pepper. Spread the pastourma slices over the cheese evenly. Cover with the remaining tomato slices and then sprinkle the rest of the cheese on top. Season with additional pepper.

4. Top the pie with the remaining 3 sheets of phyllo, brushing each with butter. Trim the edges. Score into serving pieces and bake for about 45 minutes, or until the phyllo is golden and the cheese melted.

VARIATION

Slit the pockets of 4 large pieces of pita bread without pulling the bread apart completely. Brush both sides inside with a little melted butter. Spread a few tomato slices on the bottom, season with salt and pepper, sprinkle with $1/4$ cup cheese, top with 3 slices of pastourma, a few more tomato slices, and another $1/4$ cup cheese. Press together so that the pita is flat and the filling compact. Melt a tablespoon or two of butter in a 10-inch nonstick skillet and lightly fry the pita over medium-low heat until golden and glistening and the cheese has melted. Continue with the remaining 3 pies in the same way. Let them cook for a minute, cut each into 2 to 4 equal pieces, and serve.

Leek and Seafood Pie

The combination of leeks and seafood works surprisingly well. Here is another idea culled from my weekly restaurant outings, this one to Kollia's Taverna in the boondocks of Piraeus, where he serves a similar pie, one of dozens of seafood mezethes in his repertory.

MAKES ABOUT 24 PIECES

$\frac{1}{2}$ medium octopus (see step 1 on page 159 to wash and clean)

$\frac{1}{2}$ cup extra virgin Greek olive oil

6 cups coarsely chopped leeks (approximately 3 medium), whites and tender parts of the greens

1 pound small shrimp, shelled and deveined (approximately 2 cups)

$\frac{1}{2}$ cup finely chopped fresh mint

$\frac{1}{2}$ cup snipped wild fennel or dill

$1\frac{1}{2}$ cups (about $4\frac{1}{2}$ ounces) grated Greek graviera cheese or any grated mild cheese

3 small eggs

$\frac{1}{3}$ cup milk

$\frac{1}{2}$ teaspoon grated nutmeg

Salt and freshly ground black pepper to taste

6 sheets commercial phyllo, defrosted and at room temperature

3 tablespoons nigella or sesame seeds

I. Place the octopus in a small saucepan with 2 tablespoons of the olive oil. Cover and cook over very low heat until the octopus exudes its juices and turns bright pink and tender, about 25 minutes. Remove and cool. Reserve the juices for another use (see Note).

2. Wash and drain the leeks very well. Heat 3 tablespoons of the olive oil in a large, heavy skillet and cook the leeks until wilted, about 7 minutes, over medium heat. Remove and cool slightly.

3. Preheat the oven to 350°F. Lightly oil a 9 X 13 X 2-inch baking pan. Finely chop the octopus. In a large mixing bowl, combine the leeks, octopus, shrimp, and herbs. Add the cheese. Beat the eggs and milk together, and pour into the filling mixture. Add the nutmeg, and season with salt and pepper.

4. Layer 3 sheets of phyllo on the bottom of the baking pan, brushing each with a little of the remaining olive oil. Spread the filling evenly over the surface of the phyllo. Cover with the remaining 3 phyllo sheets, brushing those with olive oil, too. Score the pie into 3-inch square pieces. Sprinkle with nigella or sesame seeds, and spray or sprinkle a little cold water over the surface of the pie. Bake for about 40 minutes in the center of the oven until the phyllo is lightly browned and the filling set. Remove, cool slightly, and serve.

NOTE

The juices are delicious as an addition to skordalia—add them while pounding. You can also use them in tomato sauces. They add a tremendous depth of flavor.

Open-Faced Chicken Pie with Mint, Feta, and Eggs

This is a modern version of a classic dish from Epirus, Greece's savory pie capital.

MAKES 8 TO 10 SERVINGS

FOR THE FILLING

3 tablespoons unsalted butter

2 large red onions, finely chopped

1 garlic clove, minced

2 cups cooked shredded chicken

$\frac{1}{3}$ cup chopped fresh mint leaves

Salt and freshly ground black pepper to taste

2 tablespoons extra virgin olive oil

$\frac{1}{2}$ pound commercial phyllo, defrosted
and at room temperature

Olive oil for brushing

2 large eggs

3 tablespoons milk

1 cup crumbled feta

I. Prepare the filling: Heat the butter over medium-low heat and cook the onions and garlic until wilted and lightly golden, or 8 to 10 minutes. In a large bowl, combine the chicken, mint, and onion-garlic mixture. Season with salt and pepper, and toss with the olive oil.

2. Preheat the oven to 350°F. Lightly oil a 10-inch-round tart pan. Place 1 sheet of the phyllo vertically in the pan. Brush with olive oil, especially around the edges. Place the next sheet on top, at a slight diagonal angle, so that it begins to form a kind of fan hanging over the circumference of the pan. Brush with olive oil and continue with remaining sheets, placing each one at a slightly different angle as you go, so that the bottom of the pan is completely covered and an equal amount of phyllo hangs over the rim.

3. Spread the filling evenly in the pan. Roll in the excess phyllo to form a rim around the pie. Beat the eggs, milk, salt, and pepper together until frothy. Mix in the feta cheese. Pour this over the pie, tilting it so that it goes all over. Bake for 50 minutes to 1 hour or until the filling is set and the phyllo golden and crisp. Remove from the oven, cool slightly, and cut from the center outward into 8 or 10 serving-size wedges.

FINGER FOODS AND FRIED TREATS

Maybe it's some primordial memory embedded in our DNA that makes us like touching food and eating small things with our hands so much. Maybe it's just that this kind of relaxed, pretense-free eating inspires conviviality, which is the very essence of the meze tradition. Whatever the reason, tidbits in all shapes, sizes, and colors, finger foods, and fried delicacies are the lifeblood of meze dining.

From crisp phyllo treats to light and puffy vegetable fritters to those irresistible Greek fried potatoes, the dishes in this chapter are all a little bit naughty. They are meant to stray from the restricted don't-eat-this and don't-eat-that track, to wander with abandon into the neighborhood of flavors and cooking techniques that let you live a little on the wild side. But that is the nature of the meze, too—after all this is a culinary tradition that evolved as an accompaniment to drinking. It is meant to bring pleasure and to give the green light to at least a little harmless indulgence. Meze food is party food.

Many of the finger foods in the meze repertory are indeed fried. Greeks almost always fry with olive oil. I have no qualms about promoting this practice to American cooks. I would even venture to say that if you invested in a bottle or two of good Greek olive oil—which means almost any brand out there at remarkably reasonable prices—the habit of frying in olive oil wouldn't break the bank. The average cost of a liter of excellent quality extra virgin Greek olive oil, at this writing, is about $8.

Foods deep-fried, panfried, or sautéed in olive oil taste great. You don't have to use extra virgin olive oil if it's too expensive; virgin or pure olive oil works just fine in the skillet and even in the deep-fryer. What you want to avoid, however, regardless of the oil you ultimately choose, is the continuous reuse and reheating of the oil. You can store used olive oil in a jar in a dark, cool place and use it once or twice more within a day or two.

Sweet-Salty Roasted Walnuts

2 cups shelled walnuts

1 tablespoon salt

2 tablespoons sugar

I. Using a wooden spoon, stir the walnuts and salt together in a nonstick skillet over very low heat for 6 or 7 minutes, or until the walnuts feel oily to the touch and emit a pleasant, nutty aroma.

2. Add the sugar. Continue stirring for another 7 or 8 minutes, or until the sugar caramelizes and the nuts begin to clump together. Remove immediately.

3. Serve the walnuts warm or let them cool on a sheet pan lined with parchment paper and then store them in an airtight container in a cool, dark place.

GREEK NUT AND DRIED FRUIT MIXES

Greeks, inherently sociable people, enjoy ad hoc get-togethers. There is always something on hand to munch on, from the simplest bowl of olives to more complicated dishes, served up in small portions as a meze. Dried fruit and nut mixes are standard fare for drinks among Greeks, and there are many combinations. Among them are pine nuts and raisins; roasted salted almonds and raisins; roasted chickpeas (*stragalia*) and chopped dried figs; and shelled salted pistachios and chopped dried apricots. ✳

Lightly Salted Dried Figs with Oregano

This is a specialty of Kalamata, a lovely home-grown treat savored during the olive harvest, when the weather turns cold and people light their fireplaces for the first time during the year. Most home cooks sun-dry their own figs—Kalamata and its environs are one of the major fig-growing regions of Greece—then roast them in embers. If you have a fireplace you may do this, too. Just wrap the figs in aluminum foil and place them under the embers for a few minutes.

MAKES 6 TO 8 SERVINGS

3 tablespoons salt

2 pounds dried Greek figs, preferably dark Kalamata figs

2 teaspoons dried oregano

$\frac{1}{2}$ teaspoon freshly ground black pepper (optional)

I. Preheat the oven to 350°F. Place 8 cups of water in a large pot. Toss in the salt. Bring to a rolling boil. Add the figs to the pot and blanch for 5 minutes until plump and softened. Remove and drain.

2. Place the hot figs on a large sheet of parchment paper. Sprinkle with the oregano and a little pepper, if desired. Wrap in the parchment, then in aluminum foil to form a tightly closed parcel. Bake the figs for 20 minutes. Serve warm.

NOTE

You may also roast the figs in a home smoker. Once they are blanched, drain them well and place them on a rack inside the stovetop smoker. They are lovely smoked over cherrywood smoking chips.

Greek Fries

Tempers run high like a vat of hot oil when it comes to discussing a properly fried potato.

The Greek fried potato is a national treasure! It is even defined on a website called the Official French Fries Pages. On another site filled with global fried potato recipes, the Greek version was described as usually cut round, always fried in a skillet, in olive oil, and served with salt and oregano. There is even an inchoate movement among culinary preservationists at the Greek National Tourist Organization for making it de rigueur for any restaurant that claims to serve traditional Greek cuisine to list fried potatoes on the menu.

Every connoisseur (and there are many) has his or her own philosophy when it comes to making perfect fries. I bow to my husband, Vassilis Stenos, who makes the best fried potatoes on earth, an art he learned from his grandmother, who lived to be ninety-eight. In the interest of saving our national treasure, I share the family recipe.

One caveat passed down from generation to generation: Never refrigerate potatoes before frying them because the starch in them converts to sugar and burns. Wash the potatoes and dry them very well before adding them to the skillet. Make sure they are all cut about the same size so that they cook evenly.

Yukon Golds or White Rose potatoes, peeled and cut into thick pieces, roughly the size of a woman's index finger

Olive oil for frying

Salt

Oregano

Grated kefalotyri cheese

Absolutely *no* lemon

Blot the potato pieces dry. Heat about an inch of olive oil in a large, heavy skillet and drop as many potatoes as will fit in one layer in the pan. Cover and sweat the potatoes in the oil over low heat until they begin to turn golden. Remove the cover, raise the heat to high, and carefully turn the potatoes, preferably 1 piece at a time, continually until they are a beautiful golden brown. Remove with a slotted spoon and continue until all the potatoes are fried. Serve sprinkled with salt, oregano, and grated cheese. Do not squeeze lemon juice over them, as this will soften the fries and all your careful work at the skillet will be for naught!

Panfried Wrinkled Black Olives with Onion, Oregano, and Garlic

Panfried olives are a classic meze for ouzo, and a specialty of the central part of mainland Greece. In other places, such as Crete, olives are often roasted or grilled, and also served up as a savory accompaniment to Greek eau-de-vie. This dish brims with color and makes a wonderful starter.

MAKES 6 TO 8 SERVINGS

1/4 cup extra virgin Greek olive oil

1/2 pound wrinkled black olives, preferably Greek throumbes

1 large red onion, halved and cut into thin half-moon slices (about 3 cups)

1 garlic clove, minced

1 teaspoon dried Greek oregano

2 tablespoons red wine vinegar

1 Belgian endive or radicchio, cut into 1/4-inch strips

2 small hard-boiled eggs, peeled and quartered

3 radishes, sliced into 1/8-inch rounds

Salt to taste

1. Heat the olive oil in a large, heavy skillet and add the olives. Sauté over medium-high heat for about 3 minutes, turning with a wooden spoon. Add the onion and sauté all together, stirring frequently, for about 7 minutes. Add the garlic, reduce the heat to medium-low, and continue cooking until the onion is very soft and very lightly browned. Mix in 1/2 teaspoon of the oregano and the vinegar. As soon as the vinegar sizzles, remove the skillet from the heat.

2. Remove the fried olives and onion with a slotted spoon and reserve the pan liquids. Place the olive and onion mixture in the center of a serving bowl, with the Belgian endive or radicchio leaves all around it. Place the hard-boiled eggs and radishes decoratively around the bowl. Pour over the pan juices, season the greens with salt, and sprinkle with the remaining oregano.

VARIATION

The same dish may also be prepared with cracked green olives seasoned with lemon.

Panfried Jumbo Olives Stuffed with Greek Fish Roe

There is something innately alluring about popping an olive into one's mouth, and savoring all the succulent brininess before washing it down with something to drink. The allure is all the greater if the olive is stuffed and savory, and if its soft, smooth skin is improved upon by the addition of bread crumbs that sizzle as the olive fries, creating a whole world of textures and flavors in a single, tiny bite. This recipe is great party food. It is the brainchild of a friend and chef, Lefteris Lazarou.

MAKES 32 OLIVES, OR ABOUT 8 SERVINGS

½ pound jumbo or extra-large green pitted or unpitted olives, preferably Greek

⅓ cup homemade taramosalata (page 27) or commercial taramosalata

½ cup all-purpose flour

1 large egg, lightly beaten

½ cup fine bread crumbs

Olive oil for frying

I. If using unpitted olives, pit them with an olive pitter to keep them intact.

2. Have the taramosalata ready. Using a pastry bag outfitted with a nozzle small enough to fit into the cavity opening of the olive, stuff each olive with the taramosalata.

3. Spread the flour onto one plate and the bread crumbs onto another. Heat about ½ inch of olive oil in a large, heavy skillet over a medium flame. Roll the olives in the flour, then in the egg, and finally into the bread crumbs. Fry over moderate heat until the bread crumbs have turned golden. Remove, place on paper towels to drain briefly, and serve.

Fried Onions

This is really the simplest "meze." I sampled it at a small taverna in Pangrati, a neighborhood in central Athens. The onions came heaped on a plate, with no pretense, no fancy batter, and no fork!

MAKES 4 SERVINGS

4 to 6 small red onions, as needed

1 cup all-purpose flour

Salt

Olive oil for frying

Red wine vinegar

1. Peel the onions. Cut them into rings about ⅛ inch thick. Place them in a bowl and toss them with the flour and salt.

2. Heat 1 inch of olive oil over medium heat in a wide pot or deep skillet. Scoop up a handful of the onions, shake off the excess flour, and drop in the oil. Fry until golden and soft. Drain on paper towels and repeat with the remaining onions. Serve, sprinkled with a few drops of vinegar and additional salt if desired.

Feta Saganaki with a Sesame-Seed Crust

Saganaki is a two-handled shallow skillet with a rounded perimeter, and any food cooked in it takes on its name. So, saganaki as a recipe includes many things. It can be a bubbling shrimp or mussel dish with spicy tomato sauce and melted cheese; it can be one of many flour-dusted panfried cheeses, too. This recipe is a take on the fried-cheese tradition, and one that began to make its way onto Athenian menus in the late 1990s. I like the contrast in textures, the crunchiness and subtle flavor of the sesame seeds next to the intenseness and softness of the feta as it is heated.

MAKES ABOUT 16 PIECES

1/4 **pound hard Greek feta or telemes cheese, aged in tins, not barrels**

1 large egg

1 cup sesame seeds

1/4 **cup extra virgin olive oil for sautéing**

2 tablespoons unsalted butter

I. The feta should be a rectangular, not triangular, piece. Cut it into four 1/2-inch slices and cut each slice into quarters to get bite-sized rectangles.

2. Beat the egg lightly in a shallow bowl. Spread the sesame seeds onto a large plate. Dip the cheese in the egg and then in the sesame seeds. Heat the olive oil and butter in a large, heavy, nonstick skillet. Place about 6 of the cheese pieces in the skillet, and sauté over medium-high heat. As soon as the feta begins to soften, flip it over to brown on the other side. Remove and serve hot. Repeat with the remaining feta and sesame seeds.

Cheese Croquettes with Graviera, Kefalotyri, and Parsley

Cheese croquettes are a big hit at tavernas and meze eateries all over Greece. Greeks love cheese; they indulge their passion liberally. Try using a wok instead of the usual skillet to fry these in. You will use less oil and the heat distribution is better.

MAKES ABOUT 36 PIECES, ABOUT 1½ INCHES IN DIAMETER

½ to ¾ cup all-purpose flour, plus 1½ cups for dredging

½ teaspoon baking powder

2 eggs

1 cup (1½ to 2 ounces) grated Greek graviera or kasseri cheese, or other mild sheep's milk cheese

1 cup (about 2 ounces) grated Greek kefalotyri cheese, or other hard sheep's milk cheese

½ cup finely chopped fresh flat-leaf parsley

Salt and freshly ground black pepper to taste

Olive or other vegetable oil for frying

I. Combine the flour and baking powder. With an electric mixer, lightly beat the eggs. When frothy, add the flour mixture and beat until combined and smooth. Add the cheeses, parsley, salt, and pepper. Taste and adjust the seasoning with additional salt, if necessary.

2. Spread about the 1½ cups flour onto a large plate or piece of parchment paper. Take 1 tablespoon at a time of the cheese mixture and shape into a small patty or oblong croquette. Dredge in the flour.

3. In a large, heavy skillet, heat about ½ inch of oil until hot but not smoking. Place 3 or 4 croquettes (or as many as will fit easily without crowding) into the hot oil and fry until golden, turning so that they cook on all sides. Remove, drain on paper towels, and serve hot. Repeat with remaining croquettes, replenishing the flour and oil as needed.

Greek Fish Croquettes

Fish patties and croquettes are a great way to use leftover fish. Serve these golden croquettes with one of the skordalia recipes (pages 25, 26, and 28), or with the mayonnaise-based dipping sauce here. It might come as a surprise that Greeks use mayonnaise at all. They do, and many cooks make their own.

MAKES ABOUT 20 PATTIES

FOR THE MAYONNAISE

½ teaspoon dry mustard

½ teaspoon sugar

½ teaspoon salt

½ teaspoon freshly ground white pepper

½ teaspoon white wine vinegar

2 egg yolks

1⅔ cups extra virgin olive oil

Juice of 1 large lemon

FOR THE FISH PATTIES

10 scallions, whites and tender green parts only, finely chopped

3 cups cooked, shredded white-fleshed fish, such as cod, snapper, or perch, all bones and skin removed

¼ cup chopped fresh wild fennel, fennel fronds, or dill

¼ cup chopped fresh flat-leaf parsley

2 tablespoons ouzo

2 scant tablespoons ground cumin

1 teaspoon grated nutmeg

Salt and freshly ground white pepper to taste

2 eggs

Flour for dredging

Olive or other vegetable oil for frying

I. Prepare the mayonnaise: In the bowl of a food processor, pulse the dry ingredients together to combine. Add the vinegar and egg yolks, and pulse until smooth. Drizzle in the olive oil, drop by drop, pulsing until the mixture begins to thicken. Then, alternate between the lemon juice and oil, pulsing on and off until the mayonnaise is emulsified and creamy. If it curdles in the process, start over with the dry ingredients, vinegar, and egg yolks, and add the curdled mixture to the new batch as it begins to thicken. Continue mixing in the lemon juice and oil, alternating between each. Store, covered, in the refrigerator until ready to use, up to 1 day.

2. Prepare the patties: Place the scallions in the bowl of a food processor and pulse until very finely chopped. Add the shredded fish and herbs, and pulse on and off to combine. Add the ouzo, cumin, nutmeg, salt, and pepper, and pulse a few more times. Add the eggs and continue processing until the mixture is smooth and dense. Transfer to a bowl and store, covered, in the refrigerator for 1 to 2 hours, or until the mixture stiffens a bit.

3. Place about 1½ cups flour on a plate or piece of parchment paper. Remove the fish mixture from the refrigerator. Take a heaping tablespoon at a time and shape into a small patty, about 2 inches in diameter. Dredge lightly with flour.

4. Heat about ⅓ inch of oil in a heavy skillet. The oil should be hot, but should not reach the smoking point. Place the first 4 or 5 patties in the oil to fry. Flip them with a slotted spatula when the bottoms are golden. Fry on the other side, remove, and drain on paper towels. Skim off the burnt flour from the flour in the skillet, and repeat with the remaining patties.

Batter-Fried Mussels

All sorts of mussel dishes are considered classic mezethes. I like these batter-fried mussels, a recipe from northern Greece that bespeaks Anatolian roots. They disappear in no time from most meze spreads. People pop them into their mouths like candy. Serve them with any of the arugula salads, with the spicy bulgur-lentil salad, and with any of the skordalia recipes in this book. They are also very good with the tarator sauce that appears on page 50.

MAKES 4 TO 6 SERVINGS

30 mussels in the shell or frozen and precleaned

FOR THE BATTER

$\frac{1}{2}$ to 1 cup all-purpose flour as needed

$\frac{1}{2}$ teaspoon salt

$\frac{1}{2}$ tablespoon baking powder

1 large egg

2 heaping tablespoons good-quality tomato paste

$\frac{1}{2}$ cup water

Olive or other vegetable oil for frying

I. If using unshelled mussels, scrub them very well and remove their little beards. Place in a steamer with 2 inches of water, cover, and steam for 5 to 7 minutes, or until the mussel shells open. Remove and drain. Discard any mussels whose shells have not opened. Remove the mussels from their shells and set aside. If using frozen, shucked mussels, defrost and rinse them.

2. Make the batter: Combine $\frac{1}{2}$ cup of the flour, salt, and baking powder in a small bowl. In a separate bowl, beat the egg slightly with a fork. Dilute the tomato paste in the water and mix this into the egg, stirring well to combine. Add the dry ingredients, mixing to form a thick batter. If it is too thin, add a little more flour as you stir. The batter should be the consistency of loose custard.

3. Heat 3 inches of oil in a large, deep skillet. Mix the mussels into the batter. Remove 1 at a time with a slotted spoon and drop into the hot oil. Fry about 7 or 8 mussels at a time. They will take just a few seconds to turn golden. Remove and drain on paper towels. Serve them hot, accompanied by the walnut-yogurt skordalia on page 26.

Deep-Fried, Breaded Cheese-Stuffed Eggplant

This is one of the many classic mezethes that evince the Greeks' love affair with cheese-filled finger foods. In a break with tradition, though, I have found that the best tool for frying these eggplant fritters is, of all things, a Chinese wok.

MAKES ABOUT 24 PIECES

4 large eggplants, washed and patted dry

1 cup extra virgin olive oil for brushing eggplant slices

FOR THE BÉCHAMEL

1 tablespoon unsalted butter

1 tablespoon all-purpose flour

1 cup whole milk

½ teaspoon salt

FOR THE FILLING

1 cup (about 3 ounces) coarsely grated Greek kasseri cheese

1½ cups (about 6 ounces) grated Greek feta

1 large egg yolk

Freshly ground black pepper to taste

FOR THE BREADING

1 cup milk

2 large egg yolks, lightly beaten with 2 tablespoons water

2 cups fine plain bread crumbs

Olive or other vegetable oil for frying

I. Preheat the oven to 400°F. Line 2 sheet pans with parchment paper and brush generously with olive oil. Using a sharp, serrated knife, cut off the stem and a little of the base of the eggplants. Hold the eggplant upright and slice into ¼-inch-thick slices, taking care to keep the slices whole and straight. Place the eggplant slices in a single layer on the sheet pans. Brush the tops generously with olive oil and bake for 10 to 15 minutes, turning once, or until softened and very lightly browned. Do not let the eggplants overbake or crisp in the oven. You might have to bake the eggplant slices in batches.

Roasted Walnut–Filled Prunes in Bacon Blankets

This recipe hints at the dried fruit-and-nut combinations that Greeks love so much. It makes a lovely accompaniment to sweet liqueurs, Greek tsipooro, grappa, and other eaux-de-vie.

MAKES 8 TO 12 SERVINGS

24 large, pitted prunes

$1\frac{1}{2}$ cups dry red wine

$\frac{1}{2}$ teaspoon cracked black peppercorns

24 walnut halves

24 thin strips of Canadian bacon or pancetta

6 slices whole-wheat bread, crusts removed, cut into quarters

I. Place the prunes in a bowl and marinate at room temperature with the wine and peppercorns for 6 hours. Remove and drain. Preheat the oven to 350°F. Butter a stainless-steel baking pan, large enough to fit the bread squares in one layer.

2. Stuff each of the prunes with one walnut half. Wrap one strip of bacon around each prune and place each piece on one of the bread quarters. Secure with a toothpick. Place the prunes in the pan and bake for about 15 minutes, or until the bacon has crisped and the bread is golden.

VEGETABLE AND
BEAN MEZETHES

Vegetables on the meze table can be simply prepared, but they have to be intense of flavor. It is no surprise that the vegetable dishes for which Greek cuisine is known and loved tend to be absent from the traditional meze palette of dishes. Sure, you can serve a small plate of stewed green beans or okra, or a dollop of spinach-and-rice pilaf, but these luscious, slow-cooked, one-pot vegetable and bean stews, whose main flavor component comes from olive oil, generally fall into the category of main courses in Greece. They aren't snappy enough to be savored in the playful spirit of meze. They don't have that necessary "edge"—mezethes are meant to entice, not to sate.

Vegetables that *are* perfectly suited as mezethes include those that are sun-dried, marinated, pickled, preserved, fried, and stuffed. Robust bean dishes are also part of the colorful spread of small plates that make up a typical meze meal. Many vegetables appear in the chapter on fried and finger foods, because they seem more fitting there. Others, obviously, are salads.

Some of the best vegetable mezethes don't have to be made at home at all. Good-quality dried tomatoes and eggplant, marinated or pickled artichokes, roasted red peppers, pickled beets, stuffed baby eggplants, and other similar treats make excellent fare, coupled with some cheese, olives, and bread, or with a meat or seafood dish. I have included only one recipe for a preserved vegetable in this chapter because it is very easy to make. There are all sorts of great artisanal preserves now being produced in Greece and exported, and many of these are perfect for a meze buffet.

By far the most popular vegetable meze dish is the platter of sliced, flour-dusted fried zucchini and eggplant that is de rigueur on practically every Greek restaurant menu the world over.

These are also quick dishes that you can make at home, too. There are two basic schools of thought regarding fried vegetables—some cooks favor a full-fledged batter, others just a simple dusting of flour. I prefer the simple flour version. The end result is less filling, certainly less stodgy. Usually fried vegetables are served with a tangy dipping sauce, such as skordalia or tzatziki, so the extra density of a batter is not necessary.

Eggplants and zucchini are two of the most versatile vegetables, and so are the main ingredients in many other mezethes as well. Greeks like to stuff eggplants with everything from bulgur (page 122) to onions to ground meat to quails. In fact, stuffed eggplants are one of the few *lathera*—olive oil–based dishes—that are often served as a meze. Eggplants with feta or with yogurt are very popular in Greek mezethopoleia (meze restaurants); stuffed zucchini blossoms are considered a spe-

cial, seasonal treat. Peppers—colorful, flavorful, and spicy—also make their appearance among the heady, bright vegetable offerings. Fried peppers, whether hot or sweet; roasted red peppers, especially the long, horn-shaped Florina variety; pepper spreads and stuffed peppers are all favorite and classic mezethes, perfect matches to strong liqueurs like ouzo, grappa, tsipouro, and the like.

Beans are also savored, and the beans that reign over all others are the large, ecru-colored butter beans—*gigantes*—one of the classics of the Greek table. There are dozens of ways to prepare them. They may be simply boiled, dressed with olive oil, lemon, sea salt, pepper, and oregano, and served as a side dish to small fried fish or grilled octopus. Or, as in the recipe in this chapter, they may be braised together with heady, robust ingredients, and stand on their own as a mainstay of the meze table.

Fried Peppers Preserved in Olive Oil

My friend Bobby, who owns Nychterida (The Bat), a historic restaurant in Hania where Anthony Quinn danced in *Zorba the Greek,* makes these peppers several times a year and reserves them for good friends. He serves them with local Cretan firewater.

MAKES 8 TO 10 SERVINGS

3 pounds long green Italian frying peppers

Olive oil for frying

Salt

4 large garlic cloves, thinly sliced

1 cup good-quality red wine vinegar

Extra virgin olive oil for preserving the peppers

I. Wash and pat dry the peppers. Pour enough olive oil into a 12- or 15-inch skillet to cover the surface by about ⅓ inch. Place enough peppers in the skillet to cover the surface in one layer. Cover the skillet and cook the peppers over low heat for 10 to 15 minutes, turning once until the peppers are lightly golden and puffy on both sides. Remove with a slotted spoon and let cool. Repeat with the remaining peppers, replenishing the oil if necessary as you go.

2. When the peppers are cooled, carefully peel away their puffy, loosened filmlike skins. Try to do this without ripping the peppers.

3. Place the peppers in a 2-quart jar in layers and sprinkle each layer with salt and garlic. Pour in the vinegar. Fill the remaining space in the jar with olive oil, close the jar, turn to combine, and let stand for at least one day before serving. Store in a cool, dry place.

Batter-Fried Zucchini Flowers Stuffed with Cheese

This is a meze for what the Greeks would call a *merakli,* someone who really knows how to enjoy his food and wine. Golden-orange zucchini flowers can be confusing to cooks unfamiliar with them. There are the female flowers, which come attached to the zucchini and get mushy when cooked, and the male flowers, which come attached to the stems. The male flowers are better to use, but they can probably be found only through specialty produce vendors or at farmstands.

MAKES 10 SERVINGS

20 male zucchini flowers

$\frac{1}{2}$ cup (about 4 ounces) soft Greek myzithra or farmer's cheese

$\frac{1}{2}$ cup (about 2 ounces) finely crumbled feta cheese

$\frac{1}{2}$ cup (about $1\frac{1}{2}$ ounces) grated Greek kefalograviera or other mild, semihard sheep's milk cheese

Freshly ground black pepper to taste

Pinch of cinnamon

Pinch of cayenne pepper

$1\frac{1}{3}$ cups water

1 cup all-purpose flour

$\frac{1}{2}$ teaspoon salt

Olive or other vegetable oil for frying

I. Gently rinse the flowers under cold water. Pat them dry carefully with a kitchen towel. Set aside for a few minutes.

2. Combine the cheeses, pepper, cinnamon, and cayenne in a bowl, and mash well with a fork so that everything is thoroughly combined.

3. Cut away the stems on the flowers, being careful not to tear the base. Fill each flower with 2 to 3 teaspoons of filling without overstuffing them. Leave enough room at the top of the flower to be able to fold it or twist it closed. Gently pinch the tops together and twist, then fold over to seal.

4. Place the water in a medium bowl and sift the flour into it, stirring all the while so that it doesn't lump. Season with salt. The batter should be very thick, like yogurt.

5. Pour about 1 inch of oil into a large, heavy skillet and heat it over a high flame. Using a spoon or your fingertips, dip the stuffed zucchini flower into the batter. Carefully drop a few flowers at a time into the hot oil, turning them gently with a slotted spoon to fry on both sides. Remove after a minute or two, as soon as the flowers are crisp and golden. Drain briefly on paper towels and serve.

Springtime Stuffed Artichokes with Citrus-Saffron Sauce

12 large artichokes

Juice of 1 lemon, plus 1 cut lemon

FOR THE FILLING

6 tablespoons extra virgin olive oil

4 scallions, finely chopped, including as much of the upper green tops as possible

1 small fennel bulb, trimmed and finely chopped (about 1 cup)

1 small carrot, pared, trimmed, and finely chopped (about $1/2$ cup)

$1/3$ cup Carolina rice

1 fresh or defrosted frozen cod fillet, from any other white-fleshed fish, shredded or finely chopped and bones completely removed

$3/4$ cup white wine

Salt and freshly ground black pepper to taste

1 cup mixed finely chopped fresh herbs: mint leaves, dill, parsley, and wild fennel

FOR THE SAUCE

1 tablespoon unsalted butter

1 tablespoon flour

1 cup vegetable broth or stock

$1/2$ teaspoon saffron threads

$1/2$ cup warm water

$1/3$ cup fresh orange juice

Juice of 1 lemon

Salt and freshly ground black pepper

1. Clean the artichokes: Fill a large bowl with cold water and squeeze the juice of 1 lemon in it. This is the acidulated water necessary to keep the artichokes from turning brown.

2. Using a sharp, serrated knife, cut off the stem of each artichoke at the base, so that it can stand upright. Lay the artichoke on its side, hold it from the stem end, and cut through at about $1\frac{1}{2}$ inches from the base. Discard all the upper leaves. Using the same knife, and holding the artichoke the same way, trim around it to remove the tough outer leaves from the bottom periphery, the way you might trim the crusts off bread. Immediately take a teaspoon and scrape out the hairy choke. Rub the artichoke with the cut lemon and drop the artichoke into the acidulated water. Repeat with the remaining artichokes.

3. Heat a large pot of lightly salted water. When it comes to a rolling boil, add the artichokes and blanch to soften, about 8 minutes. Remove and drain.

4. Heat 3 tablespoons of the olive oil and sauté all the vegetables together until soft. Rinse and drain the rice and add to the vegetables. Turn to coat in the oil. Add the fish. Add the white wine and $\frac{3}{4}$ cup water. Season with salt and pepper. Cover and simmer over low heat until most of the water has been absorbed by the rice. The mixture should not be completely dry. Remove. Mix in the herbs.

5. Preheat the oven to 350°F. Lightly oil an ovenproof glass or earthenware baking dish large enough to hold all the artichokes.

6. Fill the artichokes with the rice mixture and place in the pan. Add enough water to come about one-third inch up the artichokes. Cover and bake for 20 to 25 minutes, or until the rice is completely cooked and the artichokes tender.

7. In the meantime, make the sauce: Melt the butter over low heat in a medium saucepan. When the butter melts and the bubbling subsides, add the flour. Stir with a wire whisk or a wooden spoon until the flour is smooth and pasty and has turned a light golden color. Pour in the vegetable broth or stock, saffron, water, and citrus juices. Season with salt and pepper. Raise the heat to medium and stir until the sauce has thickened to the consistency of a loose gravy. Remove. To serve, place one or two artichokes on each serving plate and spoon the sauce over and around them.

Panfried Eggplant with Crumbled Feta

Eggplants with feta are found in tavernas and prepared at home with equal gusto. You don't even have to follow through on the last step—broiling the dish so that the cheese melts. Once the eggplants are softened in the skillet you can serve them, warm or at room temperature, with feta crumbled on top.

MAKES 8 SERVINGS

2 medium eggplants, washed and cut into ¼-inch rounds

Salt

½ cup extra virgin olive oil

1½ cups (about 6 ounces) crumbled Greek feta

Freshly ground black pepper to taste

Paprika to taste

3 to 4 tablespoons chopped fresh flat-leaf parsley to taste

I. Place the eggplant slices in a colander in layers and salt each layer. Place a plate or other weight on top and press down. Let the eggplants drain for 1 hour. Rinse in the colander and pat dry very well.

2. Heat 2 tablespoons of the olive oil in a large nonstick skillet. Place the eggplant slices in the skillet. Fry until lightly golden on both sides, turning once in the process. Repeat with the remaining eggplant slices and olive oil.

3. Preheat the broiler. Place the eggplant slices on an ovenproof platter, sprinkle with the crumbled feta, pepper, and paprika and place under the broiler, about 8 inches from the heat source, for a few minutes until the feta starts to melt. Sprinkle with parsley and serve hot.

VARIATION

Combine 1½ cups thick Greek or Mediterranean-style yogurt or drained plain yogurt (see page 51) with 2 finely chopped garlic cloves and 2 tablespoons olive oil. Season with some salt. Forgo the broiler and the feta. Once you fry the eggplant slices, place them on a platter around the yogurt, and sprinkle with parsley. Serve.

Giant Beans Baked with Roasted Red Peppers and Pastourma

Giant beans in some form or other are never absent from Greek meze menus. The key to making this dish taste as good as possible is to use high-quality roasted sweet peppers preserved in extra virgin olive oil. I usually make my own oil, and have them on hand. All you need to do is roast the peppers whole under the broiler, let them cool, peel them, and store them in a container in the fridge covered with good olive oil. You can pour a few tablespoons of the pepper-infused oil into the baking dish for added flavor. As for the beans themselves, the trick is to get the texture right. Giant beans need first to be soaked, then boiled, and finally baked. Once done, they should be soft, almost buttery, without being baked to the point that they fall apart.

MAKES 4 TO 6 SERVINGS

½ bag (¼ pound) Greek giant beans or butter beans

½ cup water

3 tablespoons plus ½ cup extra virgin Greek olive oil

1 large red onion, finely chopped

1 large garlic clove, finely chopped

4 large roasted red bell peppers, preserved in olive oil

Salt and freshly ground black pepper to taste

2 bay leaves

4 to 6 slices pastourma to taste

2 to 3 tablespoons balsamic vinegar to taste

I. Soak the beans according to package directions or in ample water for 6 to 8 hours. Remove from the soaking liquid, and place in a pot with ample fresh water (enough to come about 3 inches above the beans). Bring to a boil over high heat, then reduce the flame to low and simmer the beans for approximately 1 hour, or until al dente. About 15 minutes before removing the beans from the heat, season with salt. Drain and reserve the boiling liquid.

2. As the beans simmer, heat the 3 tablespoons olive oil in a large skillet over medium heat, and sauté the onion and garlic until translucent, about 5 minutes. Remove the peppers from their oil and finely chop. Add them to the onions and garlic, and stir over medium heat for about 3 minutes to meld the flavors a little. Remove.

3. Preheat the oven to 350°F. Place the beans and onion-pepper mixture in an ovenproof glass or ceramic baking dish. Add about ⅔ cup of the reserved bean cooking liquid, as well as 2 tablespoons olive oil and a little of the oil that the peppers were preserved in. There should be a fair amount of liquid in the dish. Season with the salt, pepper, and bay leaves. Cover the dish and bake for about 1 hour, or until the beans are very tender and their centers creamy.

4. In the meanwhile, prepare the pastourma: Cut away the *tsimeni*, or sticky spice rub, and cut the pastourma across the width of each slice into thin ⅓-inch-wide strips. Twenty minutes before the beans are done, toss in the pastourma. Five minutes before the beans come out of the oven, pour in the vinegar. Season to taste with additional salt. Remove from the oven, pour in the remaining olive oil, and serve. You can let the beans cool to room temperature as well. They also taste great the following day.

Clay-Baked Black-Eyed Peas with Peppers, Tomatoes, and Garlic

Driving around Arcadia in the central Peloponnisos one evening on my way back to Athens, I got lost and found paradise in the form of a roadside taverna where the entire family helped out and the mother cooked. One of the things she prepared was this dish, which is a local specialty. The beans should be velvety and rich with olive oil, the vegetables should melt in your mouth. All you need is a little red wine, some bread, and a small plate of these beans, and you're set.

MAKES 6 TO 8 SERVINGS

½ pound black-eyed peas

⅔ cup extra virgin olive oil

2 medium red onions, finely chopped

3 large green bell peppers, seeded and diced

2 large garlic cloves, minced

1 cup dry red wine

3 cups chopped, peeled tomatoes, preferably fresh

Salt and cayenne pepper to taste

4 to 6 tablespoons red wine or sherry vinegar to taste

I. Wash and pick over the black-eyed peas. Place them in a large pot of unsalted water and bring to a boil over high heat. Drain. Place them back in the pot with enough fresh water to cover by 3 inches. Bring to a boil over medium-high heat. Reduce the heat and simmer the black-eyed peas for about 25 minutes until they are nearly cooked. Remove and drain in a colander, reserving 2 cups of the boiling liquid.

2. While the peas simmer, heat 3 tablespoons of the olive oil in a large, heavy skillet over medium heat and cook the onions and bell peppers until they wilt and glisten. Add the garlic and stir for a minute or so. Pour in the wine. As soon as it sizzles, remove the pan from the heat. Preheat the oven to 375°F.

3. Combine the peas, the cooked vegetables and their pan juices, and the tomatoes in a clay baking dish with a cover. Add enough of the remaining water from the beans so that about 1 inch of liquid comes up over the beans. Pour in the remaining olive oil. Cover and bake for 35 to 40 minutes, or until the beans are very tender but not yet on the verge of disintegrating. Season with salt and cayenne. Taste and add enough of the vinegar to balance out the flavors. Remove from the oven, let cool, and serve.

A SEA'S BOUNTY
OF MEZETHES

Fish and seafood are absolute kings of the meze table, and the variety served up as small dishes is vast and highly regional in character. A seafood meze might be as simple as a coral-colored mountain of plain boiled shrimp, shells on, because they retain all their flavorful juices that way, or as complex as aromatic stuffed mackerel.

Fresh fish, preserved fish, all manner of fish croquettes and patties, shellfish and cephalopods all find their place in the culinary culture of mezethes.

Generally, fresh fish on the meze table tend to be small. Sardines and fresh anchovies are two of the most common and most versatile. Sardines can be fried, grilled, wrapped in vine leaves and baked or barbecued, baked with tomatoes or lemon and garlic, even stuffed. One of the great mezethes are fresh filleted anchovies marinated in citrus juices and preserved in olive oil, the Greek answer to ceviche. Other small fish, such as smelts, are fried whole and eaten whole, bones, heads, and all. You pop them into your mouth like chips.

Shellfish are another natural. There are dozens of varieties of shrimp in the Aegean, and they are usually prepared according to size. Small shrimp might go into a sauce or pie, such as the seafood pie on page 88. Medium to large shrimp are eaten whole, either grilled, sautéed in tangy sauces for the myriad dishes known as saganaki, or panfried. In the skillet and on the grill, they tend to be cooked with their shells. In preparations such as saganaki, or baked into savory, bubbling casseroles, they are usually shelled—for easier eating.

Mussels are another versatile ingredient and a favorite meze. Mussels have been cultivated in Greece since ancient times, especially along the cove-lined coasts of eastern Macedonia. Nowadays, in Greek supermarkets and fish markets, an international array of mussels is available, from the humongous—bigger than a man's ear!—mussels that come shelled and frozen from New Zealand to the small, slim local variety still farmed along the country's northeastern coast. Greek mussel recipes are almost all culled from the aromatic array of dishes that were brought to Greece itself by the Anatolian Greeks who left Turkey en masse in the 1920s, many of whom opened restaurants and mezethopoleia. To this day those are still the best places to find delicious, sweet onion-and-rice stuffed mussels; batter-fried spicy mussels (page 110); or mussels simmered in tomato sauce (page 148), all meze stars.

No mention of seafood mezethes, though, would be complete without a word on octopus. It is the quintessential Greek seafood. If the sea itself could be grilled it would taste like an octopus. On the meze table, the combination of salty-sweet, charred octopus, with its concentrated flavor, and the almost oily sweet but cooling appeal of anise-flavored ouzo works perfectly. It took me years to realize that it is not by accident that the combination pops up in regional dishes, too. Octopus dipped in ouzo is a Greek-island meze in its own right, and octopus stewed with anise-flavored fennel—the same basic duet of flavors—is a local much-loved specialty in Crete and the southern Peloponnisos.

In the recipes that follow, I have tried to present octopus and all the other seafood in ways I think will appeal to modern cooks. Seafood is such a place-specific food. All the recipes that follow bring me home to a kitchen full of memories.

Marinated Panfried Shrimp in the Shell

Along every coast in Greece there are seafood houses where one can go for a full meal of small plates or for something grander, like whole fish grilled on the bone, soups, and pastas. Regardless of whether the meal is a medley of mezethes or a full-course affair, most fish and seafood feasts start with an array of simply prepared shellfish. For Greeks that means grilled or boiled crawfish and spiny lobster, raw or steamed clams, and shrimp prepared in the shell, in any number of ways. Cooking them in the shell preserves their flavor and juiciness, although it makes for less-than-glamorous eating habits.

MAKES 4 TO 6 SERVINGS

1 pound large shrimp, unshelled

Juice of 2 large lemons

$\frac{1}{2}$ cup ouzo

$\frac{1}{2}$ teaspoon cayenne pepper

Dash of Tabasco

Flour for dredging

Salt

Olive oil for frying

1 lemon, quartered

I. Rinse the shrimp under cold water and set aside.

2. In a stainless steel mixing bowl, combine the lemon juice, ouzo, cayenne, and Tabasco. Toss the shrimp in the marinade, cover with plastic wrap, and refrigerate for at least 2 hours or up to 6 hours.

3. On a large platter, combine the flour and salt. Remove the shrimp from the marinade and turn once in the flour to dredge on both sides. Shake in the palm of your hand to remove excess flour. Place on a separate plate. While dredging the shrimp, heat about $\frac{1}{4}$ inch of oil in a large, heavy skillet. Do not let the oil smoke. Place as many pieces of shrimp as will fit in one layer in the skillet and fry over very high heat. They will need 3 to 4 minutes of total frying time; turn once so that they cook on both sides. The flour coating the shrimp will be a light golden color and the shells bright red. Remove, drain on paper towels, and repeat with the remaining shrimp, replenishing the oil if necessary. Serve hot, garnished with lemon wedges.

Shrimp in a Skillet with Creamy Tomato–Ouzo Sauce

There is this great bustling taverna in one of the northern Athenian suburbs near where we live, and this is the house special, so much so that the chef refused to give me a recipe for it. So, I deconstructed it myself only to re-create it pretty much intact. The tomatoes, cream, and ouzo make a great sauce. You could easily make a quantity and serve it over pasta. It would look and taste good with squid-ink linguine.

MAKES 6 TO 8 SERVINGS

1 pound large shrimp, heads removed and shelled but with tails attached

Juice of 1 lemon

3 tablespoons unsalted butter

1 medium yellow onion, finely chopped

1 garlic clove, minced

3 large tomatoes, peeled, seeded, and chopped

3 tablespoons ouzo

1/3 cup heavy cream

Salt and freshly ground black pepper to taste

1. Using a sharp paring knife, remove the threadlike vein from the shrimp. Wash, drain, sprinkle with lemon juice, and set aside in the refrigerator until ready to use.

2. Heat 2 tablespoons of the butter in a large skillet. When the butter stops bubbling, add the onion and cook over medium-low heat until very soft, or 10 to 12 minutes. Add the garlic and stir for a minute or so. While the onion is cooking, pulverize the tomatoes in a food processor until smooth. Add them to the skillet. Cook the tomato-onion mixture over medium heat until thick, about 8 minutes. Add the ouzo and let simmer for another 3 minutes. Drain the shrimp and add them to the skillet. Simmer for about 4 minutes, or until the shrimp firm up and turn pink. Add the cream, season with salt and pepper, and stir well but gently to combine. Just before removing from the heat, add the last dab of butter. Serve hot.

Marinated Fresh Anchovies

I could not write about mezethes and exclude this recipe. It is an absolute must on the small-plate list, albeit the version here takes a turn away from tradition with the addition of coriander and hot pepper flakes. These keep well for several days if they are sealed and refrigerated.

MAKES ENOUGH FOR 20 SERVINGS

1 pound fresh anchovies

Salt

1½ cups red wine vinegar

3 garlic cloves, peeled and cut into paper-thin slivers

1 teaspoon hot pepper flakes

½ cup chopped fresh coriander

Extra virgin olive oil

I. Clean the anchovies: Remove their heads and viscera. Hold the fish with the tail side pointing up and tug gently on one of the little tail fins, while holding the other firmly in one hand. Remove the backbone that way.

2. Place the fish in layers in a container that seals well and season each layer generously with salt. Pour in the vinegar. Cover and refrigerate for 12 hours.

3. Carefully drain the fish. Place them back in the container in layers, sprinkling a little of the garlic, hot pepper flakes, and coriander between each layer. Cover by ¼ inch with olive oil. Let the fish marinate for another 6 hours before serving. Keep the anchovies in the oil and store in the refrigerator.

FROM MEATBALLS
TO KEBABS

There are so many savory meat mezethes that choosing just a handful of them was difficult. In general meat mezethes fall into several main categories: those made with ground meat, in the form of meatballs and patties; skewered and grilled meats, either made from ground meat or from cubes mainly of pork, lamb, or chicken; and aromatic casserole-type dishes that are meant to be served on one plate and shared among the table. Greeks also relish an array of variety meats as mezethes, a custom rooted in the country's rural traditions, where people live by the dictum that nothing should ever be wasted.

Most Greek home cooks have a good hand with keftedes, the classic fried meatballs, and every one has his or her own recipe for the best. The quality of a Greek meatball is judged first by the quality of the meat, always twice ground upon request at the butcher's, but also by the juiciness of the dish. It is not unusual to combine several types of ground meat, such as pork, which is desirable because the fat content adds to the succulence of the final dish, and lamb, beef or veal, even goat.

A wide array of casseroles also find their way onto the meze platter. I have included the classic tas kebab, a specialty of northern Greece. In the ouzeries and mezethopoleia all over the country there is another meat dish called *tigania* (from the skillet), usually cubes of pork quickly sautéed with various vegetables, such as peppers, onions, and leeks.

Generally, meat mezethes are considered the most compatible with wine. Traditional meat mezethes tend to be mild, not hot and spicy. Meatballs go with wine, ouzo, tsipouro, and raki, because of their crisp exterior. Other cuts of meat, such as ribs, make an excellent choice for the meze repertory. These are casual fare, fun to eat and very versatile.

Little Meatballs Stuffed with Olives

There are many versions of stuffed meatballs in Greece. I like the contrast of the briny olives with the subtle flavor of the meat. You can also try these meatballs stuffed with small cubes of cheese, from feta to Cypriot haloumi to hard yellow sheep's milk cheeses such as kefalotyri. No matter what the filling is, just take care that it is thoroughly enclosed in the meatballs.

MAKES ABOUT 32 MEATBALLS

½ pound ground beef

½ pound ground pork

1 potato, boiled and mashed until creamy

One 1-inch thick slice of fresh rustic bread

1 large red onion, finely chopped

2 to 3 tablespoons red wine vinegar to taste

2 to 3 tablespoons ouzo to taste

1 egg, lightly beaten

Salt and freshly ground black pepper to taste

2 tablespoons dried Greek mint

35 pitted Greek green olives, preferably flavored with lemon and garlic

Olive or other vegetable oil for frying

1 cup all-purpose flour for dredging

I. Combine the ground meats in a bowl. Add the mashed potato. Run the bread under the tap and squeeze dry very well between the palms of your hands. Add to the mixture. Add the onion and 2 tablespoons each of the vinegar and ouzo. Add the egg, salt, pepper, and mint. Knead the mixture very well until everything is thoroughly combined. Add the remaining vinegar and ouzo if the mixture is dense. Cover and refrigerate for at least 1 hour or up to 3 hours.

2. Take a heaping tablespoonful of the mixture and shape into a meatball a little smaller than a golf ball. Make an indentation in the center and push in the olive. Squeeze the indentation closed and roll the meatball between the palms of your hands to shape

Grilled Ouzo–Nutmeg Marinated Back Ribs

My husband Vassilis, an artist and general Renaissance type, is the ad hoc grill man at our little summer restaurant, Villa Thanassi, on the island of Ikaria. He "developed" this dish one day out of sheer need and luck, when the restaurant was still our summer abode. One night, with little in the way of spices in the house and a carload of friends who had just arrived, he whipped this together and roasted the ribs over coals in an old stone grill. They have become a family tradition and restaurant special ever since.

MAKES 4 SERVINGS

2 pounds pork back ribs

FOR THE MARINADE

1½ cups ouzo

1 teaspoon cracked black peppercorns

Salt to taste

1 scant teaspoon freshly grated nutmeg

¼ cup extra virgin olive oil

1. Wash and pat dry the meat. Place all the ingredients for the marinade in a shallow bowl. Turn the meat in the marinade. Cover and refrigerate for 3 hours or up to 6 hours.

2. Heat the broiler or grill. Remove the meat from the marinade and grill on a rack over a pan, about 6 inches from the heat source. Brush with the marinade every 5 minutes. Grill for 10 minutes on one side, or until browned, then turn to grill on the other. Remove and serve immediately.

Spareribs Marinated in Wine, Honey, Star Anise, and Garlic

This is a Sino-Greek hybrid that came to be when our Chinese friend Bill Eng visited us from Beijing. He taught me the technique for making Chinese spareribs, which I duly co-opted and reworked with Greek wines, honey, and spices. The ribs are delicious. The sweet wine and honey cook down to a syrup, and the ribs have that intense sweet-salty coating that is absolutely addictive.

MAKES 4 SERVINGS

2 pounds pork spareribs, whole

1½ cups dry red wine

1½ cups Mavrodaphne wine

1 cup honey

6 whole garlic cloves, crushed

Two 1-inch strips of orange zest

1 star anise

1 teaspoon whole black peppercorns

Salt to taste

I. Wash and pat dry the ribs.

2. Bring the wines, honey, garlic, zest, anise, peppercorns, and salt to a boil over high heat in a wide pot. Place the ribs in the pot and bring back to a boil over high heat. Reduce to a simmer and cook until the sauce is reduced by about half. It should be thick and syrupy.

3. Light the broiler or outdoor grill. Remove the meat from the sauce and place under the broiler on a rack over a pan, about 6 inches from the heat source. Broil, turning once, until the meat is cooked through and tender and the coating very thick. Brush every 5 minutes with additional marinade as the meat broils.

Cinnamon-Scented Lamb Cubes with Tomatoes and Onions

Another classic, especially at ouzeries and mezethopoleia in Salonika.

MAKES 8 TO 10 SERVINGS

4 tablespoons unsalted butter

2 medium onions, finely chopped

3 pounds lamb, cut into stewing pieces

2 large tomatoes, grated (see Note on page 171)

1 large cinnamon stick

Salt and freshly ground black pepper to taste

$\frac{1}{2}$ to 1 teaspoon sugar, as needed

I. In a large flameproof casserole, melt 1 tablespoon of the butter and cook the onions, covered, until golden and wilted. Remove the onions from the pot and set aside.

2. Add the remaining butter, heat until it bubbles, and add the lamb. Brown on all sides. Add the onions back to the pot. Add the tomatoes and cinnamon stick, and season with salt and pepper. Cover and simmer over very low heat until the lamb is tender, about 2 hours. Add a little water if necessary during cooking to keep the contents of the pot from burning. At the end, adjust the seasoning with additional salt and pepper and a little sugar if necessary.

Skewered Ground Lamb Kebabs

Everyone loves souvlaki, the best-known Greek dish. Here, I've taken a few cues from Turkish and Armenian cooking to produce a spicy ground lamb kebab that is delicious with yogurt dips (pages 14, 16, and 17).

MAKE 6 SKEWERS

1 pound ground lamb

2 tablespoons good-quality tomato paste

3 garlic cloves, crushed

3 tablespoons extra virgin olive oil

2 heaping teaspoons dried Greek mint

$\frac{1}{2}$ to 1 teaspoon cayenne pepper to taste

Salt and freshly ground pepper to taste

1 egg white

Six 8-inch flat metal skewers

Toasted or grilled pita bread

I. Combine all the ingredients in a mixing bowl and knead very well until the mixture is compact and solid. Cover and refrigerate for 1 hour.

2. Heat the broiler or grill and lightly oil the rack on which the lamb skewers will be cooked.

3. Divide the meat into 6 equal portions and roll each into a 4-inch-long sausage. Dampen a paper towel with a little olive oil and wipe the skewers with the oil. Slip the skewers through the ground meat sausages and squeeze the mixture up and down the skewer, flattening it and pressing it to adhere to the skewer. Grill about 6 inches from the heat source for 7 to 8 minutes, turning to brown, until the meat is just cooked through. Remove and serve with pita bread and with either of the yogurt dips.

Beef Braised with Onions, Honey, and Bay Leaf

The meat in this dish turns a deep dark brown because of the honey that caramelized in the pot. It's a lovely meze. Try serving it spooned onto endive, radicchio, or Bibb lettuce leaves. It's a perfect match for some of the blended red wines that Greece is now producing.

MAKES 6 TO 8 SERVINGS

2 pounds stewing beef, cut into 3-inch squares

INDEX